本书由抖音超高人气外教大白和英语口语名师覃流星总结多年的教学教研经验精心编写而成。全书包含100个原创情景对话、100个核心习语表达及1000个高频实用例句，中外教精彩演绎，趣味讲解。同时配有外教大白的讲解音频，旨在帮助读者解决多年来英语听不懂、说不出的难题，帮助读者积累时下流行、地道纯正的英文表达，全面提升口语运用能力和思维能力，实现自信交流。

北京市版权局著作权合同登记　图字：01-2019-5178

图书在版编目（CIP）数据

你的英文说对了吗：大白外教口语天天练／（加）大白老师（Darby Hollin Cumming），覃流星著. —北京：机械工业出版社，2019.11

（优乐说英语）

ISBN 978-7-111-64259-6

Ⅰ.①你… Ⅱ.①大… ②覃… Ⅲ.①英语-口语-自学参考资料　Ⅳ.①H319.9

中国版本图书馆CIP数据核字（2019）第268942号

机械工业出版社（北京市百万庄大街22号　邮政编码100037）
策划编辑：张若男　杨　娟　　责任编辑：张若男　杨　娟
责任印制：孙　炜
北京联兴盛业印刷股份有限公司印刷

2020年1月第1版第1次印刷
169mm×229mm・13.5印张・282千字
标准书号：ISBN 978-7-111-64259-6
定价：49.80元

电话服务　　　　　　　　网络服务
客服电话：010-88361066　　机　工　官　网：www.cmpbook.com
　　　　　010-88379833　　机　工　官　博：weibo.com/cmp1952
　　　　　010-68326294　　金　书　网：www.golden-book.com
封底无防伪标均为盗版　机工教育服务网：www.cmpedu.com

PREFACE
前　言

　　大白是我在 2018 年偶然间刷抖音认识的，他在抖音上注册的名字叫二狗子。一个加拿大人取名二狗子，觉得他很有意思。我观察了他一段时间，他的视频挺有趣的，但就是一直不火，也就 2000 多个粉丝，当时我正好想找一名外教来录短视频节目，就安排人联系他来公司聊聊。

　　第一次见面，他说他在重庆一家线下机构做英语老师，平时空闲时间挺多的，所以就在网上发视频教英语，希望有人能发现他。我跟他说，我能帮助他成为拥有百万粉丝的网红英语老师，他礼貌地笑着回答："OK, sure."虽然他笑得很真诚，但眼神里还是充满了一丝怀疑。第二次见面，我给他写了几个中英双语剧本，第一个视频发出来就获得了 30 万个赞，他觉得很不可思议。第二个视频竟然达到了 100 万个赞，当晚他线下所有机构的学生都发截图给他，说他火了。那晚他的账号粉丝数涨到 30 万人，他开始觉得我对他的承诺要实现了。没过几周"大白外教英语"课程的粉丝涨到了 50 万，他说他家乡的总人口才 60 万左右，他跟妈妈说自己在中国有 50 万个粉丝，她妈妈都不敢相信。我跟他说，等课程账号的粉丝数到 100 万时，他就可以全职加入我们公司，一起为中国的英语教育做点儿不一样的事情。过了几个月，大白辞掉了线下教学的工作，加入了我们。他之前的工作只要求他每个周末去上课，周内晚上偶尔会有几个小时的课，其他时间都不用去学校，非常自由。自从入职后，跟着我们的时间上班，大白开始了"上班族"的作息表，每天拍教学视频、写剧本、写课程、录课程、和粉丝互动聊天。

　　我们作为创业公司，要求员工每周上六天班，刚开始我担心他不适应这种节奏，就跟他说他一周只需上五天班，周六可以不用来。后来他说这样对

其他人不公平，主动要求周六也来上班。作为老板，我还能说什么呢？

　　大白来自加拿大的温尼伯，一个草原上的小城市，他经常自嘲说自己是个农村 boy。当然，生活中他也保留着草原 boy 的那份纯朴，衣服只买最便宜的，买鞋也不超过 100 块钱。后来他赚得比以前多了，但依然保持简朴的生活方式，我觉得很难得。他跟我们说得最多的话就是，"要成为更好的自己，拍更有趣的视频，把课录得更好。"大白刚来公司的时候，每次刷到抖音上一些教过时的英语用法或者错误英语的老师，就特别生气，觉得他们在误导学生。而更让人生气的是，这样的老师也有上百万个粉丝。我跟他说，我理解他的感受，但我们有什么办法呢？我们能做的只有把内容做得更好，让自己更有影响力，到时再去告诉学生们，正确的英文表达是什么。对此他表示很认可，但每次看到一些乱教英文的视频也能获得上百万个赞，他依然会发给我，表示无奈。

　　在英语口语教学方面，我跟大白的理念高度一致。第一，在口语输入阶段，一定要确保你学到的是地道的英文表达，这样你说出来的英文才地道。第二，不要死记硬背单词和句子，不要做一个机械性的 talking machine。第三，除了学习语言本身，更重要的是要去了解西方的文化并学会西方人的思维模式。

　　我们想一起写一本有趣、有料、有文化的英语口语书，于是就有了《你的英文说对了吗？——大白外教口语天天练》这本书。本书包括 100 个地道的口语对话，这些全部都是我和大白原创的内容，每一个对话都反复修改过五遍以上，每一句都是时下最时尚、最地道的口语表达。只要你跟外国朋友聊天时用上这些句子，对方就会觉得眼前一亮，对你刮目相看。更重要的是，除了原汁原味的地道的英文表达，我们还配备了大白的全英文讲解，让大家在学习的过程中培养全英文思维的习惯，这也是本书最大的亮点之一。

　　相信这本书能给热爱英语的你带来不一样的学习体验和效果。

2019.10.20

To readers,

My name is Darby Cumming and I come from Canada. I'm a professional English teacher with years of experience volunteering and working in this profession.

My friend and colleague Alex and I decided to write a book designed for students who are passionate about learning English. Unfortunately many textbooks in China are outdated. Many of my students feel they are learning English that is not particularly useful in real life situations. They have trouble communicating with native speakers because English is a constantly evolving language with many new phrases and expressions.

So this book is for students who would like to learn the most local and modern English. It consists of 100 conversations, each with a new useful expression. Each conversation also uses humor and a uniquely western style of speaking so students can get a better sense of how native English speakers actually communicate.

To use this book effectively, one must first listen to the conversation. From there they can learn the intonation, pronunciation and new words. But perhaps most importantly the students should pay special attention to the English explanation of the new expression. Using English to explain English is a great way to understand the way native speakers think.

In summary, I wanted to write this book because I love living in China. Alex and I love teaching such eager students. We hope this book will allow students to learn, laugh and feel more confident in their English ability.

Darby Cumming

2019/10/16

使用说明

本书包括100个超实用原创情景对话，随学随用，激发口语表达。

Demo 朋友之间相互 Diss 的必备金句！

Hey, everybody, this is Darby. And welcome to "Speak Like a Native"!
D: Hey, man, you wanna hear me sing?
A: Uh, not really.
D: Man, I've been practicing this song all week!
A: Uh, OK. I guess so.
D: 甜蜜蜜，你笑得甜蜜蜜…… What do you think?
A: Um, don't quit your day job.
D: Shut up! You're just jealous I have such a heavenly voice.

本书包括100个时下国外超级流行的核心习语表达，纯正表达开口即说，全面提升口语运用能力。

All right, 听完今天的对话之后，我们要来学习一个非常地道的表达，叫作"don't quit Your day job"。

I really really like this expression. We always use it to diss somebody. "your day job" is how you make money, how you survive. So by saying "don't quit your day job", he's saying don't try to use singing to make money. Because if I did, try to be a singer, I would fail. In other words, he's saying I suck at singing.

"Don't quit your day job." 这句话经常用于两个朋友之间开玩笑。比如说，最近大白练习了一首中文歌，来跟我显摆，他肯定觉得自己唱得特别好。但其实我听完之后，真心觉得大白唱得很一般，所以我就跟他说"don't quit your day job"，意思是"你不要辞掉你现在的

中教外教趣味讲解，地道解读，培养英文思维能力。

工作去唱歌，如果你去唱歌的话，你会饿死"。

这个表达特别地道，如果你跟你的外国朋友说这个表达的话，他会觉得你的英文非常 native。

> 全彩大白外教漫画插图，生动形象，图文并茂助你轻松阅读。

OK, so for today's bonus. You heard me say, "You're just jealous I have such a heavenly voice."

If we think **something is amazing**, we can say, "It's **heavenly**." We **usually use this for maybe a singer's voice.** Oh, they sound heavenly. They sing so heavenly.

Or we can use this for food. You could say, "Em, this food tastes heavenly."

在今天的 bonus 当中，我们学习了一个词叫 heavenly。"**heavenly voice**" 在中文中有一个与之完美对应的词，叫作"天籁之音"。

大白在英文释义里面给大家说了，heavenly 一般用于形容两种东西：一种是 人的声音，就是你唱歌的 voice；另外一种就是 美食，觉得食物真的非常好吃就可以用 heavenly 来形容。

—Hey, boss, do you wanna hear the new song I've been practicing?
—Uh, OK.
—悄悄问圣僧，女儿美不美…
—Don't quit your day job!
—You're so mean to me!
—Haha, bye!

> 拓展内容帮助读者了解更多地道表达，是给读者真真正正的福利。

目 录

前言

To readers

使用说明

Day 1	表示"下大雨"不要再用"It's raining cats and dogs."！	/ 002
Day 2	怎么说"去吃东西"最地道？	/ 004
Day 3	cute 和 hot 这种美剧高频词应该怎么用？	/ 006
Day 4	成年人一起玩，千万不能用 play with…	/ 008
Day 5	这个看起来有语法错误的句子，居然特别地道！	/ 010
Day 6	千万不能说别人 fat，应该用哪个词描述胖呢？	/ 012
Day 7	"超级饿！"如何用英语表示才够地道？	/ 014
Day 8	"杠精"用英语怎么说？	/ 016
Day 9	"你讲真的?"用英语怎么说？	/ 018
Day 10	shit 和 the shit 居然有这么大的区别？	/ 020
Day 11	"I'm down."和"I'm feeling down."的区别是什么？	/ 022
Day 12	sick 除了表示"恶心"，还有更酷炫的意思吗？	/ 024
Day 13	"阳光男孩"不能说成 sunshine boy	/ 026
Day 14	interesting 还可以用来表示敷衍别人？	/ 028
Day 15	high 这个词，在英语中不能随便用，很危险！	/ 030
Day 16	"白头发"不是 white hair 那是什么？	/ 032
Day 17	"读懂你的小心思"，用英语怎么说？	/ 034
Day 18	千万不要说外国人的头发是 gold hair！	/ 036

Day 19	"上相"用英语怎么说呢?	/ 038
Day 20	"You're fine."和"You're so fine."意思差异居然这么大!	/ 040
Day 21	"OK."和"I'm OK."意思恰恰相反?	/ 042
Day 22	"装"用英语怎么说?	/ 044
Day 23	"Two weeks later."和"In two weeks."的区别是什么?	/ 046
Day 24	英文中也有"东施效颦"的表达?	/ 048
Day 25	美女经过不能说 pass away!那应该怎么说?	/ 050
Day 26	go out 和 go out with sb. 意思差别居然这么大!	/ 052
Day 27	"宿醉"用英语怎么说?	/ 054
Day 28	"我配不上她",一个来自棒球比赛的地道英语表达!	/ 056
Day 29	"What's up?"和"What's new?"都可以用于打招呼,区别是什么?	/ 058
Day 30	"太冷了!"的英语怎么说更地道?	/ 060
Day 31	"富得流油"用英语怎么说?	/ 062
Day 32	美国说唱歌手最喜欢的英语表达!	/ 064
Day 33	"夏天专属身材"用英语怎么说?	/ 066
Day 34	说"你疯了吗?"美国人最爱的那句是什么?	/ 068
Day 35	"史上最棒"用英语怎么说?	/ 070
Day 36	drink 在什么情况下只表示"喝酒"?	/ 072
Day 37	如何用英语表达那些"自作聪明"的人?	/ 074
Day 38	"撸铁"用英语怎么说?	/ 076
Day 39	如果你有打死都不想再见的人,这个英语表达你要 get!	/ 078
Day 40	老外怎么看待自己的年龄问题?	/ 080
Day 41	这个怼人的表达你一定要 get!	/ 082
Day 42	美国年轻人每天都挂在嘴边的一个词!	/ 084
Day 43	"无聊爆了"用英语怎么说?	/ 086
Day 44	writer's block 是什么意思?	/ 088
Day 45	如果你有了 stalker,说明你真的红了!	/ 090
Day 46	"自恋"用英语怎么说?	/ 092
Day 47	"这个男人很 man",这么说对吗?	/ 094

Day 48	"好哥们，闺蜜"英语怎么说？	/ 096
Day 49	如何用英语表达"你想都别想"？	/ 098
Day 50	我坚持学口语50天了	/ 100
Day 51	为什么北美用forever 21来回答年龄的问题？	/ 102
Day 52	如何用英语表达自己"技艺生疏"了？	/ 104
Day 53	cheap除了表示"便宜"，还能这么用？	/ 106
Day 54	"睡觉"除了用sleep表示，还可以用什么表达更地道？	/ 108
Day 55	美国年轻人口中的MIA是什么意思？	/ 110
Day 56	"怀恨在心"用英语怎么说？	/ 112
Day 57	"酒肉朋友"用英语怎么说？	/ 114
Day 58	"左右为难"用英语怎么说？	/ 116
Day 59	同样表示"再见"see you soon和see you later有什么区别呢？	/ 118
Day 60	原来salty在口语中除了表示"咸的"，还可以表示这个意思。	/ 120
Day 61	安慰别人最强有力的一句英文是什么？	/ 122
Day 62	parking ticket不是"停车票"哦！	/ 124
Day 63	喜欢喝酒的朋友们一定要知道的英文单词！	/ 126
Day 64	"摇钱树"用英语怎么说？	/ 128
Day 65	怎样用英文鼓励你的朋友去表白？	/ 130
Day 66	表达"酗酒""煲剧"用这个词更地道！	/ 132
Day 67	"扣篮"的英文居然还可以这么用？	/ 134
Day 68	"容易上当受骗的"用英语怎么说？	/ 136
Day 69	如何用interesting表达"呵呵"的意思？	/ 138
Day 70	自信的人必备的一句英文！	/ 140
Day 71	boss居然还可以这么用！	/ 142
Day 72	形容一个人状态很好可以用on fire吗？	/ 144
Day 73	shut up除了表示"闭嘴"，还有这个意思！	/ 146
Day 74	"筋疲力尽"用英语怎么说？	/ 148
Day 75	如何用英语表达"兄弟情义"？	/ 150
Day 76	"耙耳朵"用英语怎么说？	/ 152

Day 77	hook up 有这么多意思，你知道吗？	/ 154
Day 78	如何用英语表达"随大流"才够酷？	/ 156
Day 79	people person 原来是这个意思！	/ 158
Day 80	"塞翁失马，焉知非福"用英语怎么说？	/ 160
Day 81	如何用英语表达"自己对做某事非常有信心"？	/ 162
Day 82	"自我膨胀"用英语怎么表达？	/ 164
Day 83	这个夸张的英文表达你一定要学会！	/ 166
Day 84	ass-kisser 是什么意思？	/ 168
Day 85	这样表达"抢了某人的风头"非常地道！	/ 170
Day 86	nightmare 只是"噩梦"的意思吗？	/ 172
Day 87	sleep 可不只是"睡觉"的意思	/ 174
Day 88	怎样形容一个女孩美到令人窒息？	/ 176
Day 89	又一个安慰人的地道表达你一定要 get！	/ 178
Day 90	如何用英语表达"旋风式的爱情"？	/ 180
Day 91	"对某人有感觉"可以这样表达！	/ 182
Day 92	sit shotgun 这个表达非常有趣！	/ 184
Day 93	bread 和 butter 组合起来会有什么新的意思呢？	/ 186
Day 94	学会用这个表达去夸你的女朋友！	/ 188
Day 95	怎样洋气地表达"适可而止"？	/ 190
Day 96	"拜金主义者"用英语怎么说？	/ 192
Day 97	如何形容那些特别努力的人？	/ 194
Day 98	年轻人都会用到的一个表达！	/ 196
Day 99	comfort food 这个可爱的表达是什么意思呢？	/ 198
Day 100	"开心又难过"这种复杂的心情怎么表达？	/ 200

读者精彩留言　　　　　　　　　　　　　　　　　　　　　　　/ 202

Day 1

表示"下大雨"不要再用 "It's raining cats and dogs."!

A: Wow, dude, it's raining cats and dogs.
D: Man, are you my grandpa?
A: Yes, good boy.
D: Shut up, plus we don't say that anymore. We usually say **it's pouring**.
A: Let's go running in the rain. It's so romantic!
D: Uh…bye.

All right, 听完今天的对话之后，我们要来跟大家说一下"倾盆大雨"用英语怎么说。之前很多同学学到的表达是"It's raining cats and dogs."。 What do you think about that?

Yeah, when I'm teaching Chinese students, they'll often say, "Wow! It's raining cats and dogs outside." And it really does sound like I was talking to my grandparents.

Usually young people do not say "raining cats and dogs" anymore. It sounds really old fashioned. What we do say is "**It's pouring.**" "pour" means "倒" "倒给你", so **it's almost like God is pouring water down on us.**

I also just wanna add that for sure this is for north America, so Canada and the United States. Maybe in Britain they still use this expression. I'm not sure, but in north America, it's very old fashioned.

在北美地区，就是加拿大、美国，他们已经不说"It's raining cats and dogs."了，他们觉得很过时。年轻人如果想表达**倾盆大雨**的意思，就说"**It's pouring.**"，就像上帝在倒水一样。

OK, so for today's bonus. If it's pouring rain outside, often we'll say, "Don't go outside. You're gonna get **soaked**!"

What does "soaked" mean? "Wet" means you have a little bit of water on you; "soaked" means totally covered in water. Your entire body is just covered in water, to be soaked.

OK，今天的 bonus 中，我们要学习的其实是两个词：如果你的**衣服湿了**，你可以说"**we**"；但是如果你**湿透了**，就叫"**soaked**"，get soaked。

Day 2

怎么说"去吃东西"最地道?

D: Hey, man, I'm so hungry.
A: Ya, me too.
D: You wanna **grab a bite to eat**?
A: Sure. I think there's a fried chicken restaurant nearby.
D: Fried chicken? That's so unhealthy. I thought you were on a diet.
A: I don't care. I just want my fried chicken!

OK, 听完今天的对话之后,我们要学习一个非常非常地道的表达,叫"grab a bite to eat",意为"去吃点儿东西"。

"Grab a bite to eat", this is a very common expression. With my friends, maybe I would say this every day. Hey, man, you wanna go grab a bite to eat?

Now, for this expression, usually it means not to go to a restaurant and wait and have a big dinner. It usually means **to go to a fast-food restaurant**, maybe like McDonald's or KFC, **and eat quickly**.

All right, "grab a bite to eat", 这个表达真的是老外每天都会用到的,它指的是"去吃口东西"。

这个时候吃东西就不像(正式聚餐那样)我们要去一个在 fancy restaurant 吃得那么正式,而是去快餐店或者 food court, 去吃那么一口,填饱肚子。想表达"吃快餐、吃得快"的这种情景,就可以说"grab a bite to eat"。

OK, so for today's bonus. It's very important to know that for foreigners, for English speakers, when we wanna say "减肥", we say "**on a diet**". I'm on a diet.

There is another few ways that you can say this. You can say "I'm **losing weight**," "I'm trying to lose weight," or some people will say "I'm **counting calories**."

It means that they are keeping track of how many calories they lose and how many calories they take in from eating.

  今天大白给大家介绍了三种有关"减肥"的英文表达。第一个是"on a diet",就是"节食";"lose weight"是"减重、减肥"的意思;其实我个人比较喜欢第三种:"counting calories",意思是"计算自己的卡路里"。
  比如,一碗米饭多少卡路里?一根玉米多少卡路里?这个表达非常的生动和形象。当你在运动(work out)的时候就会 counting calories。

Day 3

cute 和 hot 这种美剧高频词应该怎么用？

A: Hey, man, what do you think of Angelababy?

D: Um, she's **cute**.

A: Oh, how about Shu Qi?

D: Oh, man, she is so **hot**! She is my Goddess!

A: Wow! How about Yang Mi?

D: She is hot too! She is also my Goddess!

A: Shut up!

All right, 听完今天的对话之后，我们来看一下 cute 和 hot 有什么区别。So, Darby, what's the difference between "cute" and "hot"?

Well, when we want to describe the appearance of other adults, like Angelababy, if we say "cute", it means **we recognize that they're good-looking, but maybe we're not really really attracted to them**.

But if we say "hot", that means **sexy, right? So it means maybe we really really are attracted to them. So it's a higher degree of attraction.**

OK，我来给大家用中文解释一下 **cute** 和 **hot** 的区别。在对话当中大白觉得 Angelababy is "**cute**"，说明她 good-looking，就是感官上的好看，但是他认为舒淇是他的女神，因为他觉得 she is "**hot**"，她很性感。

cute 是"感官上的好看"，而 hot 指"很性感，更有吸引力，更有感觉"。不知道大家理解了吗?

All right, it's bonus time! So for the bonus, we're gonna talk about the word "**cute**".

When we use the word cute to describe adults, it's different than when we use the word cute to describe kids and animals. For adults, of course we mean "**good-looking**" For kids and animals, it doesn't necessarily mean good-looking; it means more **adorable**. For example, maybe we want to hold a **cute** baby or pet, a really cute kitten.

对于很多中国学生来说，**cute** 都意为"可爱的"，但是我们在用 cute 形容成年人和小孩/小动物的时候，其实是有区别的。

cute 在形容成年人的时候，表示 good-looking，是"好看的"意思，但是在形容小朋友或者小动物的时候，则是"可爱的"意思。

Day 4

成年人一起玩，千万不能用 play with…

A: Hey, dude, tonight I'm gonna play with my friends.
D: Oh, how old are they?
A: Same as me. We used to be classmates.
D: Oh, you mean you're gonna **hang out** with your friends.
A: Why can't I say play?
D: In English, usually kids and animals play. Adults hang out.
A: Oh, learn something new every day!

OK，听完今天的对话之后，我们一起来看一下。在我跟大白讲我要跟我的朋友一起玩的时候，我说 I'm gonna play with my friends，但是大白却好奇我朋友的年龄。他要给大家来解释一下什么时候可以用"play with"，什么时候不可以。

Thank you, Alex. In English if you say "I'm gonna play with you", and you're both adults, we think it sounds really strange.

"**Play**" is a very childish word. Kids play with each other. Animals, for example, two cats, two dogs, can play with each other.

You can also say, "Let's go play football." "Let's go play video games." But you can not say, "Let's play together." We think it sounds very strange.

我听到很多中国学生把"我想跟你玩"翻译成:"I want to play with you."大白在抖音上也经常收到粉丝留言说:"I want to play with you."但是成年人之间一定不能说:I want to play with you,只能说: I want to hang out with you."一起玩"的英文表达是 hang out。

All right, it's time for our bonus. Now you heard Alex at the end of our conversation say, "Oh, learn something new every day." This is a fixed expression.

If you learn some new knowledge that you didn't know before, you can say, "Emm, learn something new every day!"

You know how we say this in Chinese, Darby? How? 涨知识!

Wow! Learn something new every day! Yeah!

OK. So I hope you learn something valuable today!

Day 5

这个看起来有语法错误的句子，居然特别地道！

D: Hey, man, are you busy tonight?
A: Nah, no plans.
D: You wanna **go watch a movie**?
A: With you? No way. I only watch movies with girls.
D: Dude, no worries. I also invited five hot girls.
A: OK, my treat!

OK, 听完今天的对话之后我们来学习一个非常地道的表达: "go watch a movie"。

"Go watch a movie." If I'm talking to my friends, I could say, "Hey, do you wanna go watch a movie?"

Now, why is it important to know this? Because many Chinese people will say, "Darby, do you want to go to the cinema?" Are you my grandpa?

Right now, we do not say "cinema". It's very old fashioned. We will just say, "Hey, you wanna go watch a movie?"

我们在课本上学到的"去看电影"是"go to the cinema",但是它比较过时了。就像大白说的,他们已经不说"go to the cinema",而用"go watch a movie"。

这个时候又有同学会问为什么 go 和 watch 可以连在一起用呢?两个动词怎么可以连在一起呢?说实话我也不知道为什么,我相信大白也不知道为什么。(大白:一点儿都不知道。)但是,这就是当下最流行的表达,学习语言就要不断地与时俱进。"go watch a movie"就是"看电影"当下最流行的说法。

OK, so for today's bonus. You heard Alex say "**my treat**". It means: **I will pay the bill**; **I will pay the money**. You can also say, "It's on me." They have the same meaning: it means I will pay for you.

我觉得男生什么时候最帅呢,就是当你说出这句话的时候:"My treat." "It's on me."

Day 6

千万不能说别人 fat，应该用哪个词描述胖呢？

A: Dude, your new girlfriend is so fat!
D: Man, you're so mean! Plus, she's not fat, just **big boned.**
A: No, she's just fat.
D: Come on, dude. She has a great personality.
A: Emm, interesting.

All right, 听完今天的对话之后，我们要学习 big boned 和 fat 的区别。So, Darby, what's the difference between "big boned" and "fat"?

Well, actually in the west people are very very sensitive about their bodies. We don't like to talk about appearance, and we especially don't like to tell people they're fat.

So as a very tactful way of saying somebody is **overweight**, we say: "Uh, no, **you are not fat. You are just big boned.**" It just sounds a lot nicer.

OK，在这边给大家提个醒，在跟外国人做朋友的时候，千万不要去讨论对方的体形问题。因为我们中国人特别喜欢说，"哎，你是不是变胖了？""哎，你变瘦了！"这些话都不要和外国朋友说！那该怎么说呢？要说"You look great！""You look great today！"

刚才大白跟大家说的是，如果这个女孩/男孩真的有一点儿胖，他们也不会说对方"fat"，他们会说"big boned"。

OK, time for today's bonus. As Alex said westerners are very sensitive about their weight. So we would not tell somebody they are fat. We might say: "**Oh, you are not fat. You are just big boned**."

There's another word that you can use. That word is "**curvy**". But you can not use this word to describe a guy. You can use this word to describe a girl.

If a guy is fat, maybe we would just say: "Oh, you look very strong!"

All right, 老外对体重真的是非常非常敏感。所以有另外两个词：一个叫 "curvy", 用于形容那种比较有曲线的女孩；形容男孩比较胖的，可以说 "You are strong."，你看起来非常强壮，非常"奘"。

OK. So that's it for today. Thank you so much and remember: Everyone is beautiful in their own way.

Day 7

"超级饿!" 如何用英语表示才够地道?

A: Hey, man! I'm so hungry **I could eat a horse**!
B: What? You wanna eat a horse?
A: No! I could eat a horse just means I'm really hungry.
B: Oh, I know a really nice horse meat place.
A: **Ew**, let's just eat hotpot.

All right! 听完今天的对话之后,我们要来学习一个比较夸张的口语表达,但 very native。"I could eat a horse.",我能吃掉一匹马。

So, I've heard that in Chinese, if you're very very hungry, you could say,"我可以吃掉一头牛"。But in English, we don't say,"I could eat a cow or a bull", we say, "**I could eat a horse.**" Why? I don't know. Maybe because horses are big animals and have a lot of meat you could eat.

在中文当中呢,表达"太饿了"我们一般会说,"我饿得能吃掉一头牛"。但是在英文当中,他们却说,"I could eat a horse".即"他可以吃掉一匹马"。

Hey, Alex, have a question. Why do you say "一匹马" and "一头牛"?

这是中文量词的惯用法。

Uh-oh, 以上就是今天课程的全部内容。

Bonus time! So when Alex recommended a horse place, a place you could go to eat horse, I said "ew". **When you say "ew", it means you think something is very gross or disgusting**. If I see a cockroach on the ground, I could say "ew".

　　当他们看到或者听到恶心的事物的时候，他们就会说"ew"。一般拼写为"ew"，但是这个"ew"也可以很夸张，所以你也会看到有很多个 w 的情况。

　　—Hey, Darby, you wanna go and eat some grasshoppers?
　　—Ewww!
　　—Ewww!
　　—Bye-bye!

Day 8

"杠精"用英语怎么说？

A: Dude, some haters left some rude comments on your video.
D: Ya, I saw that. Whatever.
A: It doesn't bother you?
D: No way, man. **Haters gonna hate**.
A: But one guy said you're ugly.
D: What? I'm never posting new videos again!

听完今天的对话之后，我们要学习一句网红必备语："Haters gonna hate."

Haters gonna hate, no big deal. We say this because if you're popular on the Internet, you're gonna have some people who like you, and you're gonna have some people who hate you. So when we say "**Haters gonna hate**", it means: "**Whatever. I don't care about the haters.**" Alex, Allow me to show off my Chinese.（Alex：Sure.）"不要理那些喷子！"

OK, "Haters gonna hate." 什么时候用呢？当有人在黑你的时候，就可以用到这句话。你越是有魅力，越招人嫉妒，就会有人来黑你，这个时候你就可以讲："Haters gonna hate." 不要理这些喷子，他们总会去喷别人。They're just jealous. Yeah!

OK. So for the bonus. Usually we say "Haters gonna hate", because they are just jealous, we're more popular, maybe more successful, maybe famous on the Internet, so of course people are gonna hate us. They're just jealous! Alex, allow me to show off my Chinese. (Alex: Again?) "羡慕嫉妒恨!"

All right, 今天我们的 bonus 部分和大家讲了一个词叫"jealous", 就是"嫉妒"的意思。当你的男朋友看到别的男生对你好, 别的男生给你送花, 然后跟你聊得非常开心的时候, 他特不高兴的那种感觉叫"吃醋", 你就可以说: "He is jealous." 就是"他吃醋了"。

—Hey Alex.
—What?
—You know why I never have a girlfriend?
—Why?
—Cause so many girls will be jealous!
—Shut up!

Day 9

"你讲真的？"用英语怎么说？

A: Dude, Angelababy started following you on Weibo.
D: What? **Are you for real**?
A: No. Of course not. She just followed me.
D: Seriously?
A: In my dreams.
D: Shut up!

听完今天的对话之后，我们要来学习一个非常地道的表达："Are you for real?"

Yeah, so older people in English-speaking countries might just say "Really?".

But younger people right now really like to say: "**Are you for real**?"

And you usually say it with that kind of emphasis. It just mean... Allow me to show off my Chinese: "真的假的？"

OK, "Are you for real?"就是"真的假的？"在今天的对话当中，我跟大白说，Angelababy关注了他的微博，他不是很相信，所以他就说了这句话："Are you for real?"

So it's time for our bonus. You heard Alex say: "**In my dreams**." It means "I really wish this happened, but there is no chance that it would ever happen".

Usually we say: "In your dreams!" (Alex: 想都别想!) Yeah, for example, Alex says: "I'll beat you in a badminton contest." I could say: "In your dreams! I'm way better than you at badminton."

在生活当中我们经常用这句话,"你想都别想, 不可能",就是"In your dreams"。

—Uh, Alex, I've been working really hard. 涨工资?
—In your dreams! Bye.
—Bye.

Day 10

shit 和 the shit 居然有这么大的区别？

D: Hey, bro, did you hear Eminem's last album? It's **the shit**!
A: Are you serious? I thought it was dope.
D: Ya, it's the shit!
A: What? But **shit** means it sucks, right?
D: Ya, if it sucks, it's shit, but if it's awesome, we can say it's the shit.
A: Oh, so we are the shit!

All right, 听完今天的对话之后，我们要来学习"shit"和"the shit"的区别。So, 大白, what's the difference?

OK. This is maybe really weird. If you say something "**it's shit**", it means **it's bad; it's awful.** But if you say something "**it's the shit**", it means **it's great; it means it's amazing.**

Why we say this? I honestly don't know, but you need to remember the "the". **If something is "shit", it's bad; if something is "the shit", it's good.**

OK, "It's the shit." 是当下年轻人非常喜欢的一个表达，我估计也是来自于说唱文化，some hip-hop stuff。(Darby: Ya, it comes from hip-hop.) Ya, right. 所以当你觉得某物特别棒的时候，你就可以说："It's the shit."

OK, so it's time for today's bonus. You heard Alex say that he thought that the album was "**dope**". OK, this is another word that means "**awesome**". You can say, "That party was dope." "The song is dope."

"Dope" used to mean drugs, but nowadays young people really like to say, if something is cool, it's "dope".

如果大家看一些有关说唱的电影，就是美国的一些 hip-hop 的电影，你会发现,"dope" 最开始指的是"大麻"（一种毒品）, 现在很多年轻人把它当成一个形容词: "The party was dope." 这个派对太炸了。

OK, guys, that's it for today's course. Thank you so much for listening.

If you think our course is the shit, make sure to share it with your friends, OK?

如果你觉得我们的课程特别好的话，一定要分享给你的朋友，让他们也来跟着我们一起学，Because we are the shit. We're dope!

Day 11

"I'm down." 和 "I'm feeling down." 的区别是什么？

D: Hey, bro. Jason invited us to a party.
A: Oh. You wanna go?
D: **I'm down**, you?
A: I'll pass. **I'm feeling down today**.
D: Awww, that's too bad. Hope you feel better.
A: Have a good time, bro.

听完对话之后，我们来看一下"I'm down."和"I'm feeling down."的区别。

So, Darby, what's the difference between "**I'm down**" and "**I'm feeling down**"?

Yeah, it's very strange. In English we say "**I'm down**" and "**I'm feeling down**". Both of these expressions have the word "down", but they have totally different meaning.

"**I'm down**" means **I'm willing to do something**.
— Hey! Do you wanna go watch a movie?
— I'm down!

"**I'm feeling down**", on the other hand, means **I'm in a really really bad mood**. Totally different meaning even though they both have the word "down".

All right，我来给大家解释一下"I'm down."和"I'm feeling down."的区别。 当Jason邀请我跟大白去参加party的时候，我问他愿意去吗，他说："I'm down."即他愿意去。

当表示"愿意"的时候，就说"I'm down."，相当于"I'd love to."。

当大白询问我愿不愿意去的时候，我说了一句"I'll pass."，意思是"我就不去了"。"I'll pass. I'm feeling down today.""我不去了。我的心情不好。"

OK. It's time for today's bonus. So we taught you "I'm down" means "I'm willing" or "I'd love to". We have another way of saying "I'm down". We can say "I'm up for that". I'm up for that also means "I'd love to". Very strange. I'm up for that and "I'm down" have the same meaning.

今天的bonus特别有意思，因为我们刚刚学了"I'm down."表示"我愿意"，其实有一个跟它意思相同的表达叫"I'm up for that."。不管是up还是down，都是表示"我愿意"。

Day 12

sick 除了表示"恶心"，还有更酷炫的意思吗？

A: Hey, dude, have you seen that movie *Green Book*?

D: Ya, man, that was **sick**!

A: Why did the movie make you sick? I think it was awesome!

D: Dude, me too. Sick means awesome!

A: Oh, then I could say my Prada shoes are sick.

D: Shut up! You're always showing off.

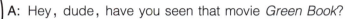

All right，听完今天的对话之后，我们要来学习 sick 在口语当中的用法。 It's very very useful!

OK. So it's important to know that "**sick**" does still mean "**ill**", to have a cold, to have a flu. You can say: Ugh, I'm very sick.

But now "sick" also has another meaning. Right now it means "**awesome**". You can say: That movie was so sick. You could also say: That party last night was so sick.

So right now "sick" has two meanings.

在我们最开始学习英语的时候，大家都知道 sick 这个词表示的是"生病的"。比如说"我生病了"，"I'm sick."。

在口语中，我们也可以用 sick 来代替 awesome，让你听起来更加地道。比如说：The party last night was sick！昨天晚上的 party 太棒了！

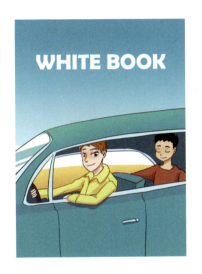

OK. It's time for today's bonus. Remember when I said "sick" had two meanings. Actually I lied. "Sick" has three meanings!

The other meaning is the same as "disgusting" or "gross". For example, if I see a cockroach on the ground, I can say：Ewww, sick! Or, for example, when I'm eating hotpot, if someone ordered duck blood, I can say：I don't wanna eat that. That's sick!

sick 在口语当中还有第三个意思，就是"恶心的"。比如，大白说如果他吃火锅的时候看到了鸭血，就会觉得 it's sick，好恶心。

Day 13

"阳光男孩"不能说成 sunshine boy

D: Hey, Alex, how are you today?
A: Great! I'm always in a good mood. I'm a sunshine boy.
D: You're a what?
A: Ya, I'm a sunshine boy.
D: Alex, we don't say that. I think you mean you're **positive** or **optimistic**.
A: Ya, I am!

All right, 听完今天的对话之后, 要给大家讲的是 sunshine boy。 为什么不能说 sunshine boy 或者是 sunshine girl, 大白?

Well, this is quite simple. It's Chinglish. In Chinese you can say you are a "sunshine" person, but in English we just don't say this. I often hear my student say: I am a sunshine girl; I am a sunshine boy. I tell them: You are **optimistic**, or you are **positive**.

以前经常听到很多学生在做自我介绍的时候说"I'm a sunshine girl."或者"I'm a sunshine boy.",自己是"阳光男孩"或者是"阳光女孩"。在中文当中我们有这种说法,但是在英文当中没有。

如果你要表示自己比较**积极向上**,你可以说:I'm a **positive** girl; I'm a positive boy.

如果你要表达你是一个**乐观的人**,就可以说:I'm an **optimistic** person.

All right. Today's bonus is quite simple. You heard Alex say:I'm in a good mood. If you are **happy**, you can say:**I'm in a good mood**. You can also say:**My mood is very good today**.

OK,今天的 bonus 就是教大家说"**我的心情很好**"的英文表达是"**I'm in a good mood.**"。

Day 14

interesting 还可以用来表示敷衍别人？

D: Hey, Alex, check out this awesome video I made!
A: Oh, it's **interesting**.
D: You don't like it?
A: What? Of course I like it. I said it's interesting.
D: But when you say interesting, you need to actually sound interested.
A: Oh! Uh, ya, it's really interesting!
D: You're so fake!

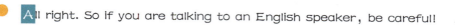

听完今天的对话之后，我们重点要讲解的就是"interesting"这个词。在最初学到这个词的时候，大家都知道，interesting 的意思是"有趣的"，但是当你用不同的语气说出这个词的时候，它却表达了不同的含义。So, Darby, how do we use it?

All right. So if you are talking to an English speaker, be careful! Because if they say 'Oh, **interesting**.", maybe they **don't care at all what you are talking about.**

So, if they say "**Wow! So interesting!**", it sounds like maybe **they really are interested.**

也就是说，我们用不同的语调说 interesting 这个词的时候，它表达的意思是截然不同的。

比如：interesting（注意听语气），这个时候你可能就是在敷衍。

但是如果你说：Wow! Interesting! 那就是真正地感兴趣，觉得很有意思。

你学会了吗？

So for today's bonus, you hear me say at the end of the conversation to Alex: **You are so fake!** It's because I can tell by the way that he is speaking that he is not being honest.

So saying "You're so fake." means you know that someone is being dishonest with you.

——Darby, You look so great today!
——Ugh, Alex, you are so fake!
——Bye!
——Bye-bye!

Day 15

high 这个词，
在英语中不能随便用，很危险！

A: Hey, dude, last night I was so **high** at Space!
D: Are you crazy? Drugs are illegal, man!
A: I don't do drugs! The club was really fun.
D: Oh, Alex, if you say you're high, it means you took drugs.
A: Oh, my God. I didn't know that!
D: Well, learn something new every day.
A: Thanks, bro!

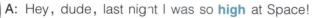

听完今天的对话之后，我们要来看一个词："high"。这个词我们在生活当中可能经常会用到。"好 high 呀！"但是，你跟外国友人在说这个词的时候要小心了。

The explanation for this is really quite simple. I know that in Chinese, people use the word "high" to mean "really excited".

But if you are talking to an English speaker, when you say "let's get **high**" or "I was so high", we will definitely think you are talking about **drugs**. "To be high" means "**to be on drugs**". So be very careful!

在今天的对话当中，我一开始说，"Last night I was so high at Space？"我想表达的是我在 Space（酒吧名）玩得非常开心，非常高兴。

但是当大白听到"high"这个词的时候，他就以为我在吸毒。因为当老外听到"high"这个词的时候，他们自然就会跟"吸毒"联系在一起。所以大家一定要注意，不要随便地用"high"这个词。

Bonus time! OK, so if you want to describe that you are very excited at a party, we have a new word that we use. The word is "lit".

You could say the bar was so lit last night. That party was lit. It means it was cool, and it was awesome. It means it was really fun. Lit!

当大家真的想要表达"这个 party 很 high"的时候，可以用"lit"这个词，这个词现在非常流行。要说这个派对特别的"high"，你就可以说：The party was lit. 但是大家要注意，不能说"I was lit."，这是不对的。

Day 16

"白头发"不是 white hair 那是什么?

A: Dude, does your dad have white hair?
D: White hair? No, he has **gray hair**.
A: I notice you have some gray hair too.
D: Shut up. I'm still young. Where's the closest mirror?
A: I'm kidding.
D: Ugh, I hate you.

All right, 听完今天的对话之后,我们要学习的是"白头发"的英文表达。如果我们直接翻译"白头发"的话就是"white hair",但是呢:

This is a really easy explanation. In Chinese you say when a person gets older, they have "white hair". In English we have "**gray hair**". So you say "white hair", we say "**gray hair**".

这个其实还蛮有趣的。 我们叫"白头发",然后他们叫"灰头发",即"gray hair"。 同时还有另外一个有意思的事情,就是外国人喝的红茶,他们不叫"red tea",而叫"black tea"。

OK, so today's bonus is why western people call the tea "black tea" and you guys call it "red tea". Well, we call it "**black tea**" because **the leaf, the color of the leaf is black**. Whereas in China you call it "**red tea**" because **the actual tea is red**.

我之前知道西方人会说"红茶"为 black tea，但是我不知道为什么。今天大白给大家解释清楚了，就是他们其实是看茶叶的颜色，而我们是看茶水的颜色。Thank you，大白。

Day 17

"读懂你的小心思",用英语怎么说?

A: Hey, dude, what's up?
D: Not much, just hanging out at my place.
A: You know, it's been a long time since we drank together.
D: Wow, you're right. It's been a whole 3 days.
A: Yeah. You wanna go to the bar?
D: Man, **you read my mind**!

All right,听完今天的对话,我们要学习一个非常地道的表达叫作"You read my mind."。

Yeah, this is a very very common expression. We say it all the time. For example, all day I'm craving, and I really really wanna eat spicy noodles, but I'm just thinking this to myself. At the end of the day, Alex says, "Hey, Darby, do you wanna go eat spicy noodles?" Wow, how did he know that's exactly what I was thinking. He read my mind.

"You read my mind."这句话翻译成中文为"你怎么知道我的想法"或者"你看透了我的心思"。比如在对话当中我问大白:"You wanna go to the bar?"(你想去酒吧吗?)他说:"Man, you read my mind!"说明他也想去酒吧,他的想法跟我一样。

再比如你特别想吃甜甜圈,这个时候你男朋友出现在你面前,拿着甜甜圈说:"想吃吗?"这个时候你就可以对他讲:"You read my mind!"你怎么知道我想吃,你真棒!

这里有一个小的细节要大家注意，这句话在口语当中一般都是<u>过去时态</u>，因为对方已经看透了你的心思，所以你要读作"You read (/red/) my mind."，而不是"You read (/riːd/) my mind."。

OK, so it's time for our bonus. And for the bonus, we're gonna teach you a cool expression, and a way to respond to "you read my mind". You can say："Well, **Great minds think alike**."

—Now, what does this expression mean, Alex? Allow me to show off my Chinese.
—Sure.
—英雄所见略同！
—Good job, bro!

All right，"Great minds think alike."这句话是用于当别人说了"You read my mind."之后的一个回应，就是"英雄所见略同"。你学会了吗？

Day 18

千万不要说外国人的头发是 gold hair！

A: Daby, I like your gold hair. I wanna dye my hair gold too.
D: What? Gold? I don't have gold hair. I have **blonde hair**. Beautiful blonde hair.
A: Oh, I wanna dye my hair blonde then.
D: Hmmm, interesting.
A: Shut up! I'll be so handsome.

听完今天的对话之后，我们要学习一个在中文和英文当中表达会有差异的短语，就是"金色的头发"。

So the explanation for this is quite simple. I guess in Chinese, you think it's "gold hair". For us we don't think the color is quite gold. We think it's more blonde, so we say "**blonde hair**". And if you have kind of blonde hair and kind of brown hair, we say **dirty blonde**.

在中文当中我们有一个表达叫"金发碧眼"，我们直接翻译"金发"就是"金色的头发"，叫"gold hair"，但是对于外国人来说，他们觉得这种颜色其实还没有那么"金"，他们把这种颜色叫作"blonde"，所以是"blonde hair"。

So for the bonus I'll teach you something interesting. Especially when talking about girls, you can say she is a blonde, or you can say she is a brunette. Of course **blonde** means she has **light hair. Brunette** means she has **dark hair**, either black or brown.

So you could ask somebody: What kind of girls do you like? Do you like blondes or brunettes?

Personally I like brunettes because I think Chinese girls are the most beautiful girls in the world.

　　Oh, my God. Darby, you are so sweet！今天我们的 bonus 当中学了两个词。
　　第一个是 blonde，它不仅仅指的是这种金头发，它还指"金发的美女"。
　　然后，如果是"黑头发，或者是棕色头发的美女"呢，就叫 **brunette**。
　　但是大家注意了，在大白解释的过程当中，提到了 light hair，译为"浅色头发"，而"深色头发"则是 dark hair。

Day 19

"上相"用英语怎么说呢？

A: Darby, I saw your new video.
D: Oh, did you like it?
A: Yes. But I think you look better in real life.
D: Ugh, I know. It's so annoying. I'm not **photogenic** at all.
A: Well, I am.
D: Shut up!

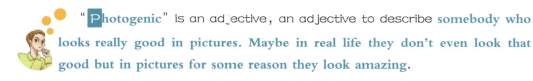

Well, 听完今天的对话之后，我们要来学习一个非常地道的表达，就是"上相"。"上相"用英语怎么说呢？

"Photogenic" is an adjective, an adjective to describe **somebody who looks really good in pictures. Maybe in real life they don't even look that good but in pictures for some reason they look amazing**.

Some people are not photogenic. They look really good in real life, like me. I'm pretty handsome.（Alex：Shut up!）But in pictures I don't look as good as I do in real life.

photogenic 就是指的"非常上相的"。比如你的好朋友给你看 ta 的写真集，你就可以说：You are so photogenic！作为好朋友 ta 肯定说：那我真人不好看吗？

实际上大部分时间"You are photogenic."都是用来夸赞别人的，夸别人非常上相，拍照片很好看。

OK, so for today's bonus we are gonna teach you a really interesting and very very local expression. We say: "**The camera adds ten pounds**."

You might realize this too. **In pictures sometimes you look fatter than you do in real life**. I don't know why. For example, Alex and I have been going to the gym for two hours every day. We are really thinner than we were before, but people will still say, "你们胖了吗?"

　　OK, the camera adds ten pounds. 虽然我们已经经常去健身了，但是当在视频里出现的时候，还是会显得很胖。视频不同于拍照，照片可以用软件修一下脸，视频没有办法修，这让我们感到很苦恼。"The camera adds ten pounds." 的意思就是"镜头会让你的脸显得你胖十磅"。

Day 20

"You're fine." 和 "You're so fine." 意思差异居然这么大！

D: Dude, I'm nervous about my interview.
A: It's OK! You are so fine!
D: What? Do you know what that means?
A: Yeah, I mean don't worry. It'll be OK.
D: Oh, actually here the word "so" makes a difference. "**You are fine.**" means don't worry. "**You are so fine.**" means…haha, you are hot!
A: Well, you are.
D: Shut up.

All right, 听完对话之后，我们今天要讲的是 "**You are fine.**" 和 "**You are so fine.**" 的区别。

So, Darby, what's the difference between "**You are fine.**" and "**You are so fine.**"?

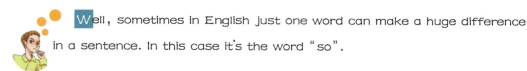

Well, sometimes in English just one word can make a huge difference in a sentence. In this case it's the word "so".

When we say "**You are fine.**", it means the same as "**Don't worry. It'll be OK. You got this.**"

But if you add "so", "**You are so fine.**", all of a sudden it means "**I think you are sexy.**", "**I think you are hot.**". So many song lyrics have "You are so fine.". It means "I really like you. You are sexy."

All right，听完大白的解释之后，我来给大家说一下："You are fine."指的是"你 OK 的、你没问题的、不用担心"。但是"You are so fine."意思就是"你很性感"。

我跟大白每天都会教大家一个在书本上学不到的地道口语表达。大家一定要记得多跟读，多模仿。

All right. Bonus time!

OK. As a bonus, let's talk about the word "fine". The word "fine" can change meaning depending on the situation.

For example, I could say："Ah, **the weather is fine** today." In this case it means **the weather is nice**, **the weather is good.**

But, for example, if my boss says："You have to work overtime!" I could say："**Oh, fine!**" It means：**I'll do it, OK, but I'm not happy.**

今天的 bonus time 我们讲到"The weather is fine."指的是"天气真的很好"，这个时候 fine 的意思就是"真的很好的"。

当你老板让你加班的时候，你偷偷地说了一个"Fine."，这个时候的 fine 就是你咬牙切齿地说："好吧。"

Day 21

"OK." 和 "I'm OK." 意思恰恰相反？

D: Hey, Alex, wanna coffee?

A: I'm OK.

D: All right! I'll be right back.

A: Man! Where is my coffee?

D: What? You said you were OK!

A: Yeah. "OK" doesn't mean "yes"?

D: Oh, "**OK**" means "yes", sure. But "**I'm OK**." here actually means "No, thanks".

A: Then give me your coffee!

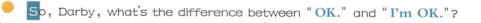

听完对话之后，我们一起来看一下"**OK.**"和"**I'm OK.**"的区别。

So, Darby, what's the difference between "**OK.**" and "**I'm OK.**"?

Well, Alex, this is another example of how in English sometimes one word can make a huge difference.

If you say "**OK.**", it means **sure, yes**, but if you say "**I'm OK.**", it actually means "**No, thanks**". So be careful!

在对话当中大白问我要不要喝咖啡，如果我想喝的话，我就得说"Yes, please."，或者是"OK."。但是我说了一个"I'm OK."，在这个地方的意思是什么呢？ 就是：No，thanks！

所以大家一定要注意：当你想喝的时候，你就说"Yes, please."，或者是"Sure, thanks."。

"I'm OK."在口语中其实是表示委婉地拒绝对方的意思。

So it's time for today's bonus. We already taught you that a polite way to refuse someone is to say "I'm OK.". Well，there are two other ways. You can say "I'm good."，and you can say "I'll pass.".

除了"I'm OK."之外，你还可以用"I'm good."，"I'll pass."来委婉地拒绝对方。

Day 22

"装"用英语怎么说？

A: Hey, dude, look at my new fancy car.
D: Wow, you bought a Ferrari?
A: No, I just rent it so people think I look cool.
D: You're **such a poser**!
A: So...you wanna hop in?
D: Let's go!

OK, 听完今天的对话之后，我们要学习一个非常 native 的表达，"such a poser"。

Such a poser. You are such a poser! "Poser" is someone who always pretend they're maybe richer, better, more talented than they actually are. They like to show off, like to brag, kind of like Alex. (Shut up!)

poser 的意思是"喜欢装的人"。因为 pose 是"摆姿势",poser 是"喜欢装的人"。

All right. So time for today's bonus! You heard Alex ask me if I wanna **hop in the car**. Among young people it's cooler to say "hop in" instead of "get in the car, come into the car". We just say "hop in".

"hop in" 是年轻人喜欢的一个表达,意思是"上车"。

—Hey, Alex. You wanna go for a ride?
—OK, wait! Let me call my chauffeur(司机)first.
—You're such a poser!
—Bye!
—Bye!

Day 23

"Two weeks later." 和 "In two weeks." 的区别是什么？

A: Hey, bro, I'm going to Thailand two weeks later.
D: Oh, that sounds fun, but the sentence sounds strange.
A: Why?
D: For native speakers, we would say I'm going to Thailand **in two weeks** or **two weeks from now**.
A: OK, got it. The beach is gonna be so beautiful.
D: They'll all see your dad bod.
A: Shut up.

All right! 听完今天的对话之后，我们要来学习 "two weeks later" 和 "in two weeks" 的区别。

大白，为什么这里我不能用 "two weeks later"？

Well, Alex, you can use "**two weeks later**" **if you are talking about the past**. You could say I went to Thailand three months ago and then two weeks later I went to Malaysia.

But **if we are talking about the present or the future**, we say "in two weeks" or "two weeks from now".

For example, "I plan to go to Vancouver in two weeks", or I could say "I'm going to Vancouver two weeks from now".

今天要给大家讲解的这个内容，对于很多学生来说，如果让你做选择题你可能不会选错，但是在口语当中却是你经常犯错误的一个知识点。

比如说在对话当中，我说我两周后要去泰国，"I'm going to Thailand."是发生在将来的事情，这个时候应该用"in two weeks"。那什么时候应该用"two weeks later"呢？

大白举了另外一个例子：他三个月以前去了泰国，然后两周之后又去了马来西亚，因为去马来西亚这件事情发生在过去，所以用了"two weeks later"。大家记住一点：发生在将来的事情，用"in"；发生在过去的事情，就用"later"。

OK, so it's time for today's bonus. You heard me say Alex had a dad bod. Now, what is a "**dad bod**"?

You take two words "dad" and "body" and put it together. What happens after you get married, you have kids, and you don't have so much time to go to the gym? you started to **put on some weight**. Maybe you have a **beer belly**. Maybe your body doesn't look so good.

So we call that a "**dad bod**", but "dad bods" actually became kind of popular recently because Leonardo DiCaprio, a very very famous actor, had a "dad bod".

OK，我们今天的"bonus"给大家讲了一个非常有意思的表达，叫"a dad bod"，指中年发福的身体。一般男人在结婚生子之后，生活比较稳定了，身体就开始发福，就会拥有一个"dad bod"。

Day 24

英文中也有"东施效颦"的表达？

A: Dude, people always try to copy our videos.
B: I know. But it's because our ideas are so good.
A: Ya, we're still the best.
B: Ya, we're the best. They're just **wannabe**s. They'll never be as cool as us.
A: Totally, man. Gimme five!

听完今天的对话，我们要学习一个非常洋气的词，叫"wannabe"。

What is a "**wannabe**"? Well, it comes from the words "**want to be**". **Somebody who wants to be as cool, as popular, as rich as someone else, but they never will be.** Alex, allow me to show off my Chinese. (Alex: OK.) "东施效颦！"

Good for you, Darby！"wannabe"指的是那些总想成为别人的人，但是却永远成不了别人（那样）的人。

All right, it's bonus time! Gimme five! (=Give me five!) We usually say "**give me five**" if we want **to celebrate something**. It means: **clap my hand!** Why do we say "give me five"? Well, because we have five fingers.

当你想要为某事欢呼庆祝的时候，就可以用"Give me five."，要求对方跟你"击掌"。Darby, give me five!

Day 25

美女经过不能说 pass away！那应该怎么说？

A: Hey, Darby, a really hot girl just **passed away**.

B: What? How could you be so happy about that?

A: Cus she's really hot, look!

B: Oh, she walked past us. You should say she **passed by**.

A: Oh, so what does pass away mean?

B: It means to die.

A: I don't care. She's hot.

B: What?

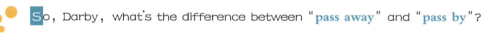

OK！听完今天的对话之后呢，我们要来学习"pass away"和"pass by"的区别。

So, Darby, what's the difference between "**pass away**" and "**pass by**"?

Well, these are two phrasal verbs using the word "pass". Phrasal verbs are very difficult in English, because they are very similar.

Now "**pass away**" means **to die**. I could say: "I'm so sorry your grandfather passed away."

"**Pass by**" means **someone or something goes past us**.

For example, that beautiful girl just passed by me, or the car just passed by me.

在今天的对话当中，我跟大白说"... a really hot girl just passed away."。"passed away"是什么意思呢？就是"去世"的意思。那我要表达的真正意思是什么呢？应该是：一个漂亮的女孩从我们身边走过。那么正确的表达我们应该说："Hey, Darby, a really hot girl just passed by."

OK, so it's time for today's bonus. As you know, "pass away" means "die", but it's very important to know that "pass away" is actually a very gentle way of saying "die". So if you go to a funeral, and you say to your friend, "I'm so sorry your mother died.", it's a little bit rude. So you could say：**I'm so sorry your mother passed away**."

OK，听完大白的解释以后不知道大家有没有了解"die"和"pass away"的区别？在中文当中，"die"相当于"死掉"，"pass away"相当于"去世"。也就是说，"pass away"是"die"的比较委婉的表达方式。我们如果说某人死掉了，这太直接太刺耳了，我们会说去世，"去世"就是"pass away"。

Day 26

go out 和 go out with sb. 意思差别居然这么大！

A: Hey, Darby, do you wanna **go out with** me?

D: What? I'm flattered, but I like girls, Alex.

A: You don't wanna go out to the bar?

D: Oh, you wanna ask me if I wanna **go out**, to hang out with you!

A: Of course!

D: But remember for next time, "do you wanna go out with me" means… "do you wanna go on a date".

A: Well, then… do you?

D: Shut up!

OK，听完今天的对话之后，我们要来学习"do you wanna go out with me"和"do you wanna go out"的区别。

So, Darby, what's the difference?

Well, when you say "**do you wanna go out with me**", this is a fixed phrase and it usually refers to "**dating**". If two people are "going out", it means maybe they are girlfriend and boyfriend.

However, "**do you wanna go out**" is usually used among friends. It just means "**do you wanna hang out**".

Hey, do you wanna go out to the bar? Do you wanna go out to the lounge?

在我们今天学习的对话当中，我想邀请大白跟我一起去酒吧，我最开始说的是：Do you wanna go out with me? 结果呢，go out with sb. 是一个固定搭配，这个搭配是"约会"的意思，只用于情侣之间。

因为我和大白是朋友关系，所以在这种情况下，我只能说：大白，do you wanna go out tonight? 你今天晚上想出去玩吗？

All right. So it's time for our bonus! You heard me say in the conversation "What? I'm flattered, but I like girls, Alex." In this situation, "I'm flattered." means "Thank you for the compliment." But "flatter" has another meaning. If you flatter somebody, for example, if you flatter your boss, it means "拍马屁".

在今天的 bonus time 当中，我们学到了一个非常地道的表达，叫"I'm flattered."。当别人夸奖你的时候，你就回应一句"I'm flattered."，相当于"您过奖了"。

Day 27

"宿醉"用英语怎么说？

D: Oh, my head hurts so much!
A: What's wrong, dude?
D: I drank too much last night.
A: So you **have a hangover**?
D: Super bad hangover. I'm never drinking again.
A: You know, Jessica is **having a party** tonight.
D: I'll be there!

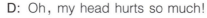

All right, 听完今天的对话之后，我们要学习一个地道的表达叫"hangover"。

Yeah, this is a very common expression. If you go out and you drink, but maybe you drink a little bit too much, the next day you'll have a **hangover**. Now this is a noun. You can also say: I'm hungover. This is a adjective（形容词）.

It basically means **maybe you have a headache, your stomach hurts, and you just feel really uncomfortable**. This is called a hangover.

OK, hangover 就是指你头一天晚上喝酒喝太多了，然后第二天起床以后的不适感，我们中文叫作"宿醉"。

OK, so it's time for today's bonus. And the bonus is really quite simple. We said in the conversation, "Jessica is **having a party**." You can also say, "Jessica is **throwing a party**." You can also say, "Jessica is **hosting a party**."

So hosting, throwing, and having a party all mean the same thing.

我们在中文当中经常说"开派对""开一个party",这个"开",很多同学就把它直接翻译成"open"。今天我们学了三个"开 party"的用法:第一个是"**have** a party",第二个是"**throw** a party",第三个是"**host** a party"。千万千万不要说"open a party"!

—Alex, do you wanna come to a party tonight?
—I'm too tired.
—Eh, there's gonna be some hot girls there.
—I'll be there.
—真香!
—Bye-bye!
—Bye!

Day 28

"我配不上她"，一个来自棒球比赛的地道英语表达！

D: Wow, check out that girl. So beautiful!
A: Dude, go ask her out.
D: Ya right? She's way **out of my league**.
A: **You're such a chicken**.
D: Why don't you talk to her then?
A: Uh, actually I already have a girlfriend.
D: No, you don't. Shut up!
A: Uh…

听完今天的对话之后，我们要学习一个非常地道的表达"out of one's league"。

Yeah, if I say that a girl is **out of my league**, it means **she is too good for me, and I'm not good enough for her**.

This actually comes from sports. In different sports, there're leagues. There's the first league, there's the second league, and there's the third league. The first league is better than the second league; the second league is better than the third league.

So if you're in the third league, and someone else is in the first league, they're better than you. So this is where the expression comes from.

OK,"out of one's league"就是指"自己配不上她(他)"或者"跟她(他)不是一类人"。

比如说刚刚我让大白去约那个女孩儿,大白说,"She is way out of my league.",就是"我根本配不上她"。

OK,for today's bonus. Sometimes in English,we use animals to represent different types of people. **A chicken is somebody who lacks courage**. "胆小鬼。"(Alex:Yeah,right. 那你都说了我没有要补充的了.)

"**You are such a chicken.**"就是"你真是个胆小鬼"的意思。

Day 29

"What's up?" 和 "What's new?" 都可以用于打招呼，区别是什么？

D: **What's up**, Alex?
A: Not much. **What's new**, dude?
D: Well, I've been to the gym more. Can you tell?
A: Yeah! You look great! You've lost some weight, right?
D: Yeah, eight pounds!
A: Wow, good for you!
D: Thanks, man!

All right, 听完今天的对话之后，我们来看一下 "What's up?" 和 "What's new?" 的区别。

So, Darby, what's the difference between "**What's up**?" and "**What's new**?"?

Well, the difference is actually quite big.

When we say "**What's up**?", we are asking "**What are you doing right now**". It's the same as "What are you up to?", "What are you doing?".

So many times people will say: Em, not much. Maybe "I'm just watching TV, playing video games". Whatever they are doing **right now**.

"**What's new**?", on the other hand, means: **since the last time I saw you, (maybe it was a month ago, two months ago), has any interesting thing happened?** Have you got engaged? Did you go to the gym and lose weight?

So actually when we say "What's new?", we want to hear some more

information. Whereas when we say "What's up?", maybe we are just saying it as a greeting.

All right, 当你听到别人用"What's up?"跟你打招呼的时候, 就可以回答 not much。它其实就是一种打招呼的方式, 对方其实并不是特别想知道你到底正在干什么 (What are you doing?)。就像我们中文中的"你吃了吗?"。对方真的是想知道你吃了吗? 或者是你吃了什么吗? 其实不是, 就是一个打招呼的方式。

但是"What's new?"着重表示一种关心, 他真的有点儿想知道你最近发生了什么事情。这就是"What's up? 和 What's new?"的区别。

So, as a bonus, we just talked that "What's up?" means "What are you doing?", but actually among young people these days, we often say "What's up?" It means the same as "hey" or "hello".

So **you can actually respond to "What's up?" by saying "What's up!"**. But this is usually just young people that say this, except for my mom will also say this, because she wants to sound young and cool.

All right, "What's up?" 在年轻人之间也被当作 hey, hello 使用。比如对方跟你说了一句"What's up?", 然后你也可以用"What's up!"来回应。刚刚大白说他妈妈也喜欢用"What's up!"来回应对方, 因为这样显得她更酷、更年轻。

—Hey, Darby, what's up?
—What's up!

"太冷了!"用英语怎么说更地道?

A: Dude, make sure to dress warm.
D: Really? Is it **cold** outside today?
A: Cold? It's **freezing cold**, man.
D: I don't need a coat if you hold me tight.
A: Get out of here!

听完今天的对话之后，我们要来学习"cold"和"freezing cold"的区别。So, Darby, What's the difference between "cold" and "freezing cold"?

Well, basically it's a different degree. If we say "cold", it means: Yeah, it's pretty cold. Maybe it's minus 10, minus 15. If we say it's "freezing cold", it means: It's very very cold, maybe minus 30.

My home town, sometimes minus 30, sometimes minus 40. That's "freezing cold".

All right, "cold"和"freezing cold"的区别：cold 就是指的(普通的)"冷"。(这两个词)指两种不同程度的冷。大白用了一个比较形象的例子，就是他的家乡温尼伯(在加拿大)的气温经常会在零下30度以下，这个时候他就会说"freezing cold"，"冻成狗"！

OK, so for today's bonus, we're gonna teach you a romantic expression. Girls, if you're really cold, you can tell your boyfriend to "**hold you tight**".

这是英文当中一句比较暧昧的话，（算是）一句情话。"抱紧我"，就是"**hold me tight**"。

Day 31

"富得流油"用英语怎么说？

A: Dude, in the future we're gonna make so much money.
D: Ya, man, we're gonna be rich.
A: Not just rich, **filthy rich**. I'll buy a Lamborghini. Girls will love it!
D: Oh, girls love me because I'm really good-looking.
A: **Go to hell**!

听完对话之后，我们要学习 rich 和 filthy rich 的区别。So, Darby, what's the difference?

OK, so again this is a difference in degree. "Rich" means **pretty rich, you got a lot of money**; "Filthy rich" means **way too much money**. In fact this is kind of a bad word. It means **you have too much money. Maybe you don't even know what to do with it**.

Someone who is filthy rich might have a huge yacht（游艇）, twenty houses ... too much!

That's our future!

OK, I'm down!

OK,是这样的:"rich"就是有钱,"filthy rich"我们可以把它翻译得直白一点儿,就是"富得流油",特别地有钱,钱多得都不知道怎么花。

OK,guys, it's time for our bonus. You heard Alex tell me "Go to hell!" It's really quite simple. This is our version of "去死".(Alex:Ya, right.) Because "hell" is "地狱", so "go to hell" means "去地狱".

——大白,跟我念:地狱.
——Whatever, I'm not Chinese. Go to hell, Alex.
——You go to hell!

Day 32

美国说唱歌手最喜欢的英语表达！

D: Hey, bro, let's get filthy rich.
A: Ya, man. We can buy whatever we want.
D: Or we can just get a bunch of bills and do what?
A: **Make it rain**! Make it rain!
D: Ya, and we'll sit in our yacht（游艇）and...
A: Stop dreaming. We got work to do.
D: Aw, OK...

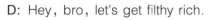

听完今天的对话之后，我们要学习一个非常"swag"（酷炫）的表达，就是"make it rain"。

"Make it rain", this is originally comes from hip-hop culture, rap culture. They really like to show off how rich they are, so they **take a lot of dollar bills and they keep it in their palm and then they**（向外抛洒纸币）, make it rain.

OK, "make it rain" 来自于说唱文化，你会看到一些说唱歌手，他们喜欢炫耀自己的财富，所以他们会**拿很多现金放到手里，然后这样……不知道大家有没有想象出来（向外抛洒）**, make it rain, **感觉像在下雨一样**, 沐浴在 dollar 的世界里。"Their money is raining in the sky.", 说明有很多钱。

OK, so it's time for our bonus. In the conversation you heard me say "We'll sit in our yacht and…" OK, what is a "yacht"? **A yacht is a huge ship that a very very rich person owns.**

In the west it's the ultimate sign that you're rich if you have a yacht. And you can invite many many famous people, beautiful people and have yacht parties. For example, "小李子", Leonardo DiCaprio, has a yacht, many beautiful girls, many parties.

All right, 在西方人的眼里，当你（具备）什么（条件）时标志着你特别有钱？比如当你拥有一艘游艇的时候。

—Alex, when are we gonna have our own yacht?
—Stop dreaming! We got work to do!
—Oh, 对对对，搬砖搬砖！
—Bye!
—Bye!

Day 33

"夏天专属身材"用英语怎么说？

D: Hey, bro, come to the gym with me. Let's lift weights!
A: Man, I'm too tired.
D: But summer is coming! We need our **beach bod**s!
A: Ugh, you're right. If I had a 6-pack, all the girls would love me.
D: Girls love me because I have a handsome face.
A: Shut up! I hate you!

All right, 听完今天的对话之后，我们要来学一个非常时尚的表达，叫 "beach bod"。

Beach bod, so this is a popular expression. When I used to live in Canada, the winter would be really long and the summer was short, but we have many beaches that we could go to.

If you go to the beach, you gotta take your shirt off. So you wanna have a **beach bod**. It means **you have muscles**. So every winter, our friends, we would say "We gotta get the beach bod ready for the summer.", but it never happened.

All right,"beach bod",在中文当中,没有对应的翻译,我们可以叫它"沙滩身材"。就是说,你在冬天的时候发福了,但是夏天要来了,"Summer is coming.",你必须把你的"beach bod" get ready。

OK,so it's time for today's bonus. I'll teach you a cool expression. But first I wanna show off my Chinese.(Alex:All right.)六块腹肌!We say a 6-pack. Or if you are really really really muscular,maybe you have a 8-pack.

—How many packs do you have?
—Ten.
—One!

All right,that's it for today's class. Thank you so much for listening. Bye.

—Let's go to the gym.
—All right.
—Actually I'm tired.

说"你疯了吗？"美国人最爱的那句是什么？

D: Hey, man, who do you think is gonna win the NBA this year?
A: Of course the Lakers!
D: **Are you insane**? They're terrible this year!
A: But they're my team!
D: Well, your team sucks.
A: Go to hell!

听完今天的对话之后，我们要学习一个非常酷炫的表达，叫作"Are you insane?"

Are you insane? OK. So maybe insane is a new word for you guys. "**Insane**" just means **crazy**; insane means **mad**.

So you can say, "Are you mad?" "Are you crazy?" But a lot of young people right now really like to say, "Are you insane?"

这句话在年轻人当中用得特别多，表示对对方的行为或者说的话不相信，就是"你疯了吗？"："Are you insane？"

比如说你的男朋友跟你分手了，然后你却还想着他，给他买东西，你的闺蜜会说："Are you insane？"即"你有病吧？"。

OK, so for today's bonus. If something is not good, and if you don't like something, you can say "it **sucks**".

The way that we use this word is：it's a verb（动词）. So something can "suck". For example："That movie sucks." "Your team sucks." It means that movie is **bad**. I don't like your team.

"suck"这个小词在口语中经常使用，电影和美剧中，很多台词都会涉及。比如"今天的天气很糟糕。"，你就可以说："The weather today sucks."

——大白，今天我们得加班！
——You suck, Alex!
——Bye!

Day 35

"史上最棒"用英语怎么说？

A: I was watching basketball last night. Lebron James is the greatest ever.
D: No way, Michael Jordan is **the GOAT**.
A: What? Michael Jordan is a goat?
D: No, he's the GOAT. Greatest of all time.
A: Oh, I see. Then we're the GOAT English teachers.
D: Ya, you're right. We're Number 1.
A: Gimme 5!

听完今天的对话之后，我们要来学习一个非常 swag（酷炫）的表达，叫"GOAT"，大写的"GOAT"。

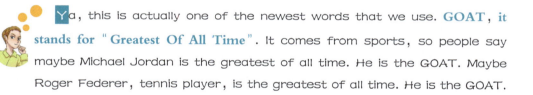

Ya, this is actually one of the newest words that we use. **GOAT, it stands for "Greatest Of All Time"**. It comes from sports, so people say maybe Michael Jordan is the greatest of all time. He is the GOAT. Maybe Roger Federer, tennis player, is the greatest of all time. He is the GOAT.

—So for English teachers, who do you think is the GOAT?
—Of course I'm the GOAT!
—What? No way. I'm the GOAT teacher!
—I'm the GOAT!
—OK, OK, OK, we are the GOATs!
—All right.

OK, so for today's bonus, we are talking about Lebron James, and we're talking about Michael Jordan. These are great players. So obviously they've won many many awards, including the MVP award.

Now what does "MVP" mean? It means "most valuable player". So for a reason if you are the best player in the league, you can be called "the MVP", the most valuable player, but also businesses might have this award. For example: Who is the MVP of "优乐说"? (Alex: Darby.) 应该是大白。(Alex: Ya, right!)

在球赛中，"MVP"就是"最有价值的球员"，在公司中就是"最有价值的员工"。比如说今年我们"优乐说"的 MVP 就应该是：(It) goes to Darby! Congratulations, man!

—Thank you. I'm so honored.
—涨工资？
—Shut up! Haha!

drink 在什么情况下只表示"喝酒"?

D: Hey, Alex, you wanna **drink**?
A: Ya! What do you want?
D: I'm gonna get some beer.
A: Cool. I'll have apple juice!
D: What? I thought we were gonna drink!
A: Ya, I'm gonna drink apple juice.
D: Uh, Alex, in English when we say let's drink or you wanna drink, it always means alcohol.
A: Oh, really? I didn't know that. One apple juice, please!
D: Oh, my God!

All right! 听完今天的对话之后,很多中国学生都会对"drink"这个词产生疑惑,因为 **drink** 在我们的认知里面就是"喝东西"的意思,可以 drink beer, drink apple juice, drink coffee 等。

但是在我们今天的对话当中,当大白问我: Hey, Alex, you wanna drink? 我说完 apple juice 之后呢,他却觉得我不应该喝 apple juice,而应该是喝酒。 大白, why?

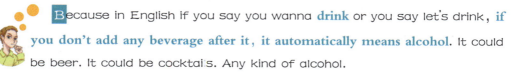

Because in English if you say you wanna **drink** or you say let's drink, **if you don't add any beverage after it, it automatically means alcohol**. It could be beer. It could be cocktails. Any kind of alcohol.

If I wanted to invite Alex to drink something else, for example, coffee, I would say: Hey, Alex, do you wanna **drink coffee**?

OK，我们来看一下原文。大白问 Alex，you wanna drink？这个 drink 单独出现的时候，他其实就是想问我想不想喝酒。

如果他想问我要不要喝别的东西，他就会在 drink 后面加上一个名词，比如说：You wanna drink water？/You wanna drink coffee？/You wanna drink apple juice？

Very good explanation, Alex! So now it's time for our bonus. There are two types of drinks. There are alcoholic drinks, and there are non-alcoholic drinks.

Alcoholic drinks contain alcohol, such as beer, cocktails, wine. **Non-alcoholic drinks do not contain alcohol**. So if you drink apple juice, of course you are not drinking alcohol.

在今天的 bonus 当中，大白给大家讲了两种饮品。第一种叫 alcoholic drinks，就是含酒精的饮品；另外一种叫作 non-alcoholic drinks，就是没有酒精的饮品。

—Hey, Alex, wanna go get some beers?
—No! I love apple juice.
—Oh, my God!

Day 37

如何用英语表达那些"自作聪明"的人？

A: Hey, man. Looks like you've put on some weight.
D: What? Really? No!
A: I'm serious. You should go to the gym more.
D: I have no time though.
A: You know, if you go to the gym, you can lose weight.
D: Wow. Thanks, **Captain Obvious**.
A: I'm just giving you some advice... fatty.
D: I hate you.

听完今天的对话之后，我们要来学习一个非常地道的表达"Captain Obvious"。

Yeah, we call somebody "Captain Obvious". If they **say something that's really really really obvious**, and it's a sarcastic comment, kind of mean to make fun of them. For example, someone could say:

—Hey, you know water is wet?

—Wow! Thanks! Captain Obvious!

OK，今天学习的这个表达其实一般用于讽刺对方。当对方说出everybody都知道的一个事情的时候，你就可以说"Captain Obvious"，翻译成中文叫"明显队长"。

OK, so for the bonus, in the conversation, you heard Alex call me a **fatty**. So if someone is fat, you can call them a fatty. I wouldn't say this to their face because it's not nice at all.

If someone's short, you can also call them a shorty. Again they probably wouldn't be very happy about this, cuz it's not very polite.

对，当你看到一个胖子的时候，你可以叫他"fatty"，就是"胖子"；如果看到一个比较矮的人，你可以叫他"shorty"。但是，如果你当面这么说，非常不礼貌。不过朋友之间开玩笑的话，还是 OK 的。

对，everybody is beautiful in their own way. You are so nice. I know.

—So what are you having for lunch today?
—KFC?
—Fatty！
—You fatty!

Day 38

"撸铁"用英语怎么说？

A: Hey, man, did you go **pump iron** at the gym?
D: Ya, I just got back.
A: Um, did you shower?
D: Uh, no. Why?
A: You smell bad, man.
D: Really?
A: Now I know why you're single.
D: No, man, some girls love my smell.
A: Oh, my God. You're **hopeless**.

All right, 听完今天的对话之后，我们要来学习一下"撸铁"用英语怎么说。

We say **pump iron**, because weights that we lift used to be made out of iron, and "to pump" means "to lift" something, something very heavy. So we say pump iron, (it means) **to lift weights**.

大白已经解释得很清楚了，所以我就不多说了。大白，what's the bonus for today?

Oh, the bonus for today! The bonus is "**hopeless**". Alex told me I was hopeless. And yes, if a guy thinks that girls like the smell of his sweat, he is probably hopeless.

"Hopeless" means **you have no chance, you are a loser, it's never gonna get better for you.**

—无药可救！You are hopeless, man!

—No, I'm cool, man.

—Yeah, you are cool.

—cool!

—Dude, did you take shower this morning?

—Man, don't you know? Canadians don't shower!

—Shut up!

Day 39

如果你有打死都不想再见的人，这个英语表达你要 *get*！

A: Hey, bro, I was with Jason last night.
D: Oh, really?
A: He said he hasn't seen you in a long time.
D: Oh, I've been avoiding him like **the plague**!
A: Why?
D: Because... I owe him money, but **I'm so broke**!
A: Get a job, you loser!

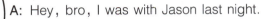

听完今天的对话之后，我们要来学习一个非常地道的表达。

To avoid somebody or something like **the plague**. What's **the plague**? The plague **is a terrible, horrible, infectious disease that spreads from one person to another and can kill you.** So you obviously want to avoid it.

So if we really want to avoid someone, for example, an ex-girlfriend, we could say: "I'm avoiding her like the plague."

Darby, you are so mean!

No, she's crazy!

OK，我们刚刚讲的这个词叫"plague"，它在中文中的意思为"瘟疫"。所以当你不想见到某人的时候，就可以用这个表达，叫"avoid... like the plague"。就像大白说的，他不想见到他的 ex-girlfriend。

All right, so for today's bonus, you heard me say "I'm so broke." So what does "**broke**" mean? "Broke" means **you have no money at all** （一点儿钱都没有）. If you are broke, you will be very sad.

"broke"就是破产了，没有钱了，穷得叮当响。"I'm broke."就是一分钱都没有了，分文没有（不名一文），一贫如洗！

OK, that's it for today's class. Have a good one, guys!

Day 40

老外怎么看待自己的年龄问题？

A: Hey, man, you're turning 30 this year.
D: Ya, in a few months.
A: Are you anxious about it?
D: No, man, not at all. Don't you know, 30 **is the new** 20.
A: So, I'm still 22.
D: Sure, but... I see some wrinkles on your face.
A: What? Shut up!

All right, 听完今天的对话之后，我们来学习一个非常酷炫的表达，叫："30 is the new 20."

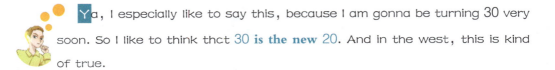

Ya, I especially like to say this, because I am gonna be turning 30 very soon. So I like to think that 30 **is the new** 20. And in the west, this is kind of true.

For example, my parents' generation, they would go to university, they would get a job, they would start working when they were like 22.

Nowadays in the west, we're encouraged during our 20s to travel, to have fun, to not worry so much.

So even from 30 to 40, we don't have to think too much, right? We don't have to work as much as maybe Chinese people do.

—You guys are so lazy.

—Ya, I can't argue with that.

OK, so it's time for today's bonus. And the bonus I think is really interesting and quite positive.

We have wrinkles, right? How do you say wrinkles in Chinese? (Alex：皱纹。) Chinese girls specially fear wrinkles, right?

In the west, we have a word for wrinkles. We say "**smile lines**". It sounds a lot nicer, because **you get wrinkles from smiling a lot. So we say they're not wrinkles. they're just smile lines**. It's very "委婉".

—That's very good to know.

—Ya, so you don't have wrinkles. It's just smile lines, cuz you're such a positive guy.

—Shut up!

—Alex, I'm gonna go put my facial mask on.

—Don't be so girly.

—Are you just jealous of my soft baby-like skin?

—Bye！

—Bye！

Day 41

这个怼人的表达你一定要 get!

D: Wow, my latest video already has 1 million likes!
A: Ya, that's because I wrote the script.
D: Are you sure? I think it's because of my good looks, man.
A: Dude, **get over yourself**!
D: Hey, man, **God's fair**. I'm not so smart so he gave me this cute face.
A: You idiot!

听完今天的对话之后，我们要来学习一个**怎么去怼你的朋友**的有意思的表达。

"Get over yourself." And we say it with that kind of tone. If **somebody is bragging or they think that they're better than other people**, we can say: Get over yourself.

For example, if I say, "Alex, I'm so handsome." (Alex: Get over yourself.) Allow me to 炫耀我的中文：自恋，narcissistic. **If somebody's being narcissistic, we can say get over yourself!**

—By the way, narcissistic in Chinese 是"自恋的".
—Uh, 好吧，反正我很帅。
—Get over yourself!

OK. Time for the bonus. I said **God's fair**. I'm not smart, so I'm good-looking. We often say this, and I think in Chinese you can say "上帝很公平". (Alex：Yeah, right.)

Some Chinese people say this to me. They say：Oh, you're so lucky. You have colorful eyes. Why people have colorful eyes？I say God's fair, because Chinese people look young.

你把我的台词全抢完了，"**God's fair**." 是"上帝很公平"的意思。

—Alex, actually I think maybe God's not fair, because he made me too handsome.
—Get over yourself. Shut up!
—Bye!
—Bye!

美国年轻人每天都挂在嘴边的一个词!

D: What do you think of the new boss?
A: I like him. He seems **chill**.
D: Ya, he doesn't seem so strict. I like that.
A: Totally. I'm gonna slack off even more now.
D: Um, bro, he's standing right behind you.
A: Uh, oh!

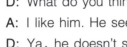

All right, 听完今天的对话之后,我们要学习一个非常 native 并且年轻人现在天天都在用的词,叫"chill"。

Chill, we use this word every day, all the time, and we use it in many different ways too.

A person can be "chill", as an adjective (形容词)。It means **really laid back, really cool, not really worried about anything**. So that's the adjective, but you can also use it as a verb. For example, "Hey, do you wanna chill?"

当"chill"形容人的时候,其实中文中没有跟它对应的翻译,可以说"ta 是一个不让人感到那么紧绷的人",就是(形容一个人)比较放松,让你感觉(跟 ta 在一起)很舒服。

当"chill"做动词的时候,它其实相当于"hang out",就是"出来一起玩一玩,放松一下"。You wanna chill?

OK, so for today's bonus, you heard Alex say "I'm gonna **slack off** even more now." "slacking off", allow me to 炫耀我的中文:"偷懒." **It means to be lazy**, especially when you are supposed to be doing something.

You could say: I should've studied last night, but I was slacking off. I should be working hard at work, but I am slacking off, maybe watching Douyin.

以上就是今天课程的全部内容,现在我可以 slack off 了,因为大白又把中文的部分全讲了。

大白:因为我的中文真的太棒了!

Shut up!

—Alex, you wanna chill tonight?
—With you? Not really, I only chill with hot girls!
—Shut up! I hate you!

Day 43

"无聊爆了"用英语怎么说？

D: Hey, man, wanna come to my place and chill?
A: And do what? Your place is **boring as hell**.
D: Come on, man. I've got a rowing machine, bro. It's so cool!
A: OK, bye!
　(sound of hanging up)
D: Who doesn't love rowing machines? Alex is so boring.

OK，听完今天的对话之后，我们要来学习一个非常地道的表达，就是"无聊爆了"。

"**B**oring as hell"，not just boring, but super, super, super boring. If you think something is **incredibly boring**, like a class or maybe a movie, you can say "It's boring as hell".

OK，如果我们要表达什么东西"无聊爆了"，就可以说"boring as hell"。比如大白邀请我去他家，他说他家里有一个rowing machine，就是"划船机"。（大白：It's so fun!）No, it's boring as hell!

OK, so it's time for today's bonus. You can add "**as hell**" to the end of many words to increase the degree of what you wanna say. For example, Chongqing. We live in Chongqing. The summer is hot as hell.（重庆的夏天太热了！）

—Oh, and I have to say：Chinese girls are hot as hell.

—你真是油嘴滑舌！

—不是，这个叫"我的嘴很甜"。

—Good for you!

—Alex, are you sure you don't wanna come to my place and use my rowing machine?

—No, thank you. It's boring as hell.

—Aw!

writer's block 是什么意思？

D: All right, let's keep writing more scripts.
A: Ya, who're the best English teachers?
D: Obviously we are, bro.
A: So, any ideas?
D: Uh, oh. You?
A: Um, let's take a break.
D: Ya, it's just **writer's block**. We're still awesome!

OK, 听完今天的对话之后，我们要来学习一个非常地道的表达，叫 "writer's block"。

Ya, **writer's block**, it's very simple. **If you have something to write, like an essay, or a book, or a script, but all of a sudden, you have no ideas, and you can't think of anything to write**, we call this writer's block.

It's especially common for authors. Sometimes they can write many many pages, and sometimes they have to take a break because they can't think of anything to write at all.

OK, **writer's block** 就是你的灵感突然被堵住了，一般是对于这些作者、作家而言，他们在写作的时候会遇到 writer's block。我跟大白有时候在写课程的时候，突然就没了灵感，我们就需要 take a break，休息一会儿。

OK, so today's bonus is super cool and super local. You heard Alex say, "Who are the best English teachers?" We are, obviously!

A more local way of saying this is "**Who da best?**" Forget about grammar. The grammar is totally wrong. We just like to say this, "Who da best?" And then you can answer it with "**We da best**".

我们的课程为什么要叫"Speak Like a Native"？（因为）这个课程讲的内容，其他的 Chinese teachers 可能讲不了。

比如说，今天要学习的"Who are the best?"。那老外在说的时候会说什么呢？"Who da best?" D-A, who da best。

这个真的不知道是什么语法，但是老外就这么说。"We da best."，等于"We are the best."，口语中简化为"We da best."。

—Who da best!

—We da best!

—Actually our students da best.

—You da best!

Day 45

如果你有了 *stalker*，说明你真的红了！

A: Wow, bro, you've got 5 million fans on Tik Tok.

D: Ya, man. But I'm kind of freaked out.

A: Why?

D: This crazy fan keeps following me. I have a **stalker**.

A: Oh, well, is she hot?

D: Dude, it's a he.

A: Uh, oh.

OK，听完今天的对话之后，我们要来学习一个只有你特别火了之后才会有的待遇，stalker！

Yeah, it's actually kind of a scary word. If you're really really famous, you probably don't want to have a stalker.

A **stalker is someone who's so crazily obsessed with someone, that they won't leave them alone.** They'll follow them. They'll go to their home. It's a little bit scary, isn't it?

"stalk"作为动词的时候是"跟踪"的意思。本意来自于那些凶猛的动物要去捕猎，然后就悄悄地跟踪其后。

"stalker"就是"跟踪者"，有时把它翻译成中文叫"私生饭"（"饭"音译"fan"，即"粉丝"），比如有一些行为过激的粉丝会跟踪明星，然后去 ta 家门口堵 ta，索要签名、拍照什么的。会做一些过激行为的粉丝就叫 stalker。

OK, so for today's bonus, you heard me say "I'm freaked out". If you wanna another way of saying scared, a more local way of saying scared, you can say "I'm freaked out".

For example, I'm scared of cockroaches, "蟑螂". If I see one in my home, it will freak me out.

"freaked out"相当于"scared"，就是"害怕，吓着了"。"I am freaked out"等于"I'm scared."。

freak out 也可以做一个动词短语来用。比如说，"那个电影把我吓坏了"，就可以说"That movie freaked me out."。

"自恋"用英语怎么说？

A: Hey, man, check out my new hairstyle.
D: Dude, you look like a rooster.
A: What? David Beckham has this haircut. I look so good.
D: Man, don't be so **narcissistic**. Beckham can pull off any hairstyle, because he actually has a handsome face.
A: Go to hell, man. I don't wanna be your friend anymore!

All right, 听完今天的对话之后，我们要来学习一个非常地道的表达，叫"narcissistic"。

"Narcissistic", it sounds very strange, right? This word actually comes from Greek, the Greek language. Narcissistic means "自恋的".
Actually it comes from a legend, where a really really handsome man, the most handsome man in the world, saw his reflection in the water in a pool. And he fell in love with his own looks, with his own face.
And so eventually, he drowned in the pond. Because he loved himself too much. So we say don't be narcissistic.

这其实来自希腊的一个神话。有一个长得特别帅的神，What's his name, Darby?（Darby: Narcissus.）他的名字叫 **Narcissus**。然后有一天，他走到了水边，看到了自己的倒影，在那一瞬间就爱上了自己，他就一直看一直看。

最后发生了什么？ What happened?（Darby: He drowned.）他淹死了！（Darby: He died.）

OK, so it's time for our bonus. You heard me say Beckham can pull off any hairstyle. What this means is that Beckham will look good no matter what kind of hair he has, because he's really handsome.

Now,"**pull off**", maybe this is a new expression. **It means that you can do something.** For example, I can say, even though I didn't study for my exam, I can pull it off, I can pass it.

But we also often use this expression for a style. For example, I can pull off having long hair. I would look super good. I mean I used to have long hair, and I was a handsome guy.（Alex：And it was ugly!）Alex could not pull it off.

OK,"pull off" 是什么意思呢?就是当你做了一种造型的时候，能不能 hold 得住（驾驭得了）。比如说他可以 pull it off，就是他可以 hold 得住。

—But Alex, I really wanna tell you when I had long hair, I was so handsome.

—Don't be so narcissistic!

Day 47

"这个男人很 man"，这么说对吗？

A: Man, I've been working out lately.

D: How's that going?

A: I've got so much muscle now. I'm so man.

D: Oh, dude, you mean you're so **manly**! Manly is an adjective.

A: Ya, I'm a manly man.

D: Oh, really? What do you think of *Titanic*?

A: Such a great movie... (Weeping)

All right，听完今天的对话之后，我们要来学习一下 manly 和 man 的区别。So，大白，What's the difference?

Yeah, a lot of Chinese, actually it's a kind of Chinglish to say "很 man"，彭于晏很 man. But actually we don't say "man". We say someone is a man.

But "**manly**" 是... How do you say that in Chinese? (Alex：很男人的。) Oh, OK, yeah, it means maybe you got lots of muscle, a low voice, um, some...

—Just like us.

—Yeah!

—Just like us. Really manly!

—We are so manly.

—So manly.

OK, so it's time for toady's bonus. Manly, a manly man, lots of muscle, low voice. And the opposite of that is to be **girly**.

Yes, so maybe some, I think some Korean actors, maybe they wear make-up (化妆) and we think they're kind of girly.

(Alex: Yeah, right. Not only in Korea.) In lots of places. And so what do you guys think? Who's a manly man? Who's a girly man?

　　—Alex, I'm so manly.
　　—Oh, really?
　　—Yeah.
　　—There's a mouse next to you.
　　—Oh! Oh, my God!

(Laughing)

"好哥们，闺蜜"用英语怎么说？

A: Hey, man, can I use your car tomorrow?
D: Sure dude, anytime.
A: Wow, thanks. You're totally my **bestie**.
D: What? We're not girls, man. You can say we're **best bros**.
A: Oh, but bestie souncs so cute.
D: Dude, grow up. You're 32!
A: No, man, I'm forever 21.
D: Shut up!

All right, 听完今天的对话之后，我们要来学习"best bros"和"bestie"。

Yeah, so if you are **a girl**, you can have a **bestie**. But if a guy says he's my bestie, it sounds very girly.（Alex：Yeah, very girly.）

So usually（between **boys**）we just say he's my bro, he's my **best bro**. Or sometimes we say, this is really "地道", we say he's my **homie**.

女生之间说闺蜜，她们会说 bestie。但男生就一般说 best bros（好哥们），或者 bro，或者是 homie。

OK, so it's time for today's bonus. Now some of our students might already know this, because our students are so smart. (Alex: Yes, so good.)

Anyway, so some girls, instead of bestie, will say "**BFF**". What does BFF stand for?

Best friend forever. Best friend forever. 永远的好朋友。

—Alex, we are homies, right?
—I'm your boss.
—Shut up!

如何用英语表达"你想都别想"?

A: Hey, bro, you wanna ask Emily out?
D: Ya, she's a total babe. But I don't think I'm her type.
A: Oh, really? Then I'm gonna go ask her out.
D: **Over my dead body**! I'm calling her right now! She'll be mine!
A: She didn't answer you. Sorry, bro!
D: Aw.

All right, 听完今天的对话之后我们要来学习一个非常地道的表达, 叫作"over my dead body"。

"Over my dead body", this means that **there's no way you're gonna let somebody do something**. It actually means you have to kill me and then walk over my dead body if you want to do this.

So in this case, I like Emily so much. She's so amazing that Alex would have to kill me to get her.

当你不想对方做某事, 或者不允许对方做某事, 就可以用这句比较夸张的表达, 叫"over my dead body"。你想干这件事, 除非你杀了我, 从我的尸体上走过去, over my dead body。

All right, so it's time for today's bonus. If you really really wanna say a girl is super sexy, there's a fixed expression. You can say she's a **total babe**. "Babe" means **good-looking girl**. Total just make the "程度"更高.

All right, 大白已经解释清楚了，我不需要多说什么了。当你觉得<u>一个女生真的非常性感、非常火辣、非常漂亮</u>的时候，你就可以说："She's a <u>total babe</u>." Darby：Total babe.

——Darby, who do you think is a total babe?
——Honestly I think every girl in China is a total babe.
——You're so fake.
——No, I mean it.
——Bye！

我坚持学口语 50 天了

Congratulations! You are halfway through the course!
A: Hey, man, this is Day 50.
D: Wow, time flies!
A: We've made it so far.
D: Ya, we totally reached a **milestone**.
A: So, let's get some beers?
D: Obviously!
A&D: Congratulations, guys!

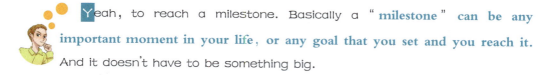

OK, 听完今天的对话之后,我们要来学习一个非常有标志性、有意义的单词,叫作"milestone"。

Yeah, to reach a milestone. Basically a "**milestone**" can be any **important moment in your life**, or any goal that you set and you reach it. And it doesn't have to be something big.

Sometimes if we ask a Chinese student what your milestone is, they'll say passing "高考" or getting married, or having a kid. But it can actually be something small too, right?

Say you're a smoker, you smoke cigarettes, and you quit, and for one week, you don't smoke, you could say, "Wow! I did it". One week, that's a milestone. So it can be big, it can be small as well.

Yeah, right。"milestone"在中文里翻译为"里程碑",像大白说的,它可以是很大的事情,比如说你结婚了,你有小孩了或者是你参加高考,这都可以是你人生的 milestone。但是也可以是一些比较小的事情,比如说你戒烟,你七天没有吸烟,这七天(的成功坚持)就是你的一个 milestone。

OK, so it's time for today's bonus. We said in the conversation "**We've made it so far**". What does it mean to make it so far?

It means that **you've persisted for a very long time.** And in this case, you've reached Day 50, so if you keep going, if you don't give up, we can say we've made it so far.

Another example could be maybe you go hiking, but the hike is 10 kilometers. So you make it 5 kilometers. You could say we've made it so far. Let's not give up. Let's keep going.

"We've made it so far."这句话一般用来给自己加油打气,就是你坚持了一件事情,做了很久,然后取得了一些成绩。

比如说,大白举了一个例子,去 hiking 的时候,(假如)一共要走 10 公里,你已经走了 5 公里了,你可以说:"We've made it so far."我们都走了这么远了,一定要坚持下去。

就像今天大家已经坚持学习到第 50 天了,我们离 100 天还会远吗?We've made it so far!Congratulations!

Day 51

为什么北美用 forever 21 来回答年龄的问题？

A: Hey, man, how old are you?
D: How dare you ask me that? It's a secret.
A: What? You're a guy and you're younger than me! I can ask you that.
D: OK, fine. I'll tell you. I'm **forever 21**.
A: 21? Then why do you have so many gray hairs?
D: It's not gray. It's blonde, okay?

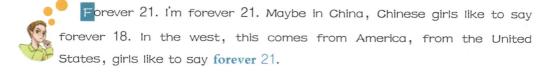

OK，听完今天的对话之后我们要来学习一个非常洋气的表达，叫"forever 21"。

Forever 21. I'm forever 21. Maybe in China, Chinese girls like to say forever 18. In the west, this comes from America, from the United States, girls like to say **forever 21**.

First of all, you shouldn't ask a girl how old she is. But if you do, she'll say forever 21. Why 21? Maybe because in the United States, that's when you are legally allowed to do many things.

For example, drinking, going to a bar. It's kind of your first year of being mature but you're also very young. So it's a good year.

在北美，当你问一个女孩儿她的年纪的时候——当然首先你不能去问一个女孩儿的年纪，这样显得你非常粗鲁——在你坚持要问的情况下，对方如果跟你很熟她就会说"I'm forever 21."，我永远21岁。

那么这个短语出自哪里呢？是因为在美国，21岁（起）可以喝酒、才

可以买酒、可以进酒吧，所以她们觉得 21 岁是一个比较重要的年纪。

再有就是在美国，当你 21 岁的时候，就可以参加很多活动。 比如说一些酒吧会专门举办一些 party 去庆祝年轻人 21 岁了。 所以你在 21 岁的时候会过得特别快乐。

这就是为什么她们会说："I'm forever 21."

OK, so it's time for the bonus. And the bonus is kind of interesting because if you ask a woman in her mid-to-late twenties or maybe thirties, she might say "I'm forever 21."

If you ask an older woman, for example, a woman my mom's age, maybe 50, 60, they can't say forever 21, but they might say **29 and holding**. It means **this birthday I'll be 29, the next birthday I'll be 29, always 29**.

今天的 bonus 也特别有意思，对于年纪稍微长一些的（女性），比如说 50 岁、60 岁，她们就不再说"forever 21"，因为显得装嫩，她们会说"29 and holding"，就是她一直在过 29 岁的生日。

    —Hey, bro, how old are you?
    —I'm 29.
    —But why do you look like you are 40?
    —Shut up!

（Laughing）

Day 52

如何用英语表达自己"技艺生疏"了？

A: Hey, everybody, this is Alex.
D: Hey, everybody, this is Darby and welcome to like a…uh… speak like a…
A: What? You **idiot**. What's wrong with you?
D: I'm not an idiot, man. I'm just **rusty**. We haven't done this for a few days.
A: No, you're just an idi…
D: Your English is rusty too… idiot.
A: Bye!

All right，听完今天的对话之后，很多同学可能以为我们没有准备好今天要讲的内容，但其实这是我们设计的一个非常完美的对话。今天我们要学习的词叫"rusty"。

"Rusty"，this is quite easy to explain. When I'm in China, my Chinese is pretty good because I'm using it every day. When I went back to Canada for a month, and then I came back to China, all of a sudden, it was very difficult to speak Chinese.

I could say, "Ugh, my Chinese is so rusty."

Another example is if I go back to Canada, and I try to skate or play hockey which is very popular in Canada. I don't skate in China, so maybe for a year I don't skate, so my skating is very poor. I fall all over the ice. You can say my skating is rusty.

"rusty"这个词是"生疏了"的意思，rust是"生锈"的意思，跟我们的中国的俗话"刀不磨，要生锈"一个道理。当你的技能，比如你的语言技能、你游泳的一些技能，变得不好的时候，可以说 rusty。

OK, so for today's bonus. We called each other "**idiots**". And actually this is very common in Canada and the United States among friends to call each other idiots. It means "大笨蛋"。

二傻子，you idiot! idiot 直接翻译成中文是"蠢货"的意思，但实际上他们不是真正地说对方是蠢货。常用在朋友之间，会说："你这个二傻子。"大概就是这个意思。

—Alex, you know who definitely are not idiots?
—I don't know.
—Our students. They're so smart.
—Good for you.
—Bye.

105

Day 53

cheap 除了表示"便宜",还能这么用?

A: Hey, man, so it's your turn to pay tonight.
D: Oh, right... uh, ya.
A: So what should we order?
D: We don't need much, right? Nobody's too hungry, right?
A: Man, you're so **cheap**!
D: I'm not cheap.... just frugal. I spend wisely.
A: Shut up! You're just cheap. Let's order drinks.
D: Ya, sure. So, water's okay, right?
A: Bye.

OK,听完今天的对话之后,我们要来学习和"cheap"意思相同的另外一种表达方式。

Ya, **cheap** actually has many meanings in English. Cheap can be inexpensive. Cheap can be bad quality. But if a person is cheap, we can also say stingy. Allow me to 炫耀我的中文,"小气,抠门".(Alex: Yeah, that's you, totally.) Yeah, totally me.

Basically, it means **somebody who doesn't want to pay**. For example, if you go to a restaurant, and maybe your bill is 100 dollars. In North America we tip(给小费). If somebody spends 100 dollars and then they tip 3 dollars, we would say "You are so cheap".

在今天的对话中,"cheap"的意思是"小气的,吝啬的"。就像大白举的例子,比如你去美国吃了一餐,花费100美金。我们之前讲过,一般是小费最少要给到餐费10%,一般会给到15%,如果你觉得他服务得特别好,也可以给到20%。

如果你吃了100美金的饭,却只给了人家3美金(小费),那个服务员估计要疯掉的。

OK, it's time for today's bonus. You heard me already explain what cheap means. What about frugal? We use the word frugal in the conversation. I'm frugal. I spend wisely.

Frugal is actually an okay word. Cheap is a bad word. Frugal is a good word. It means you... (Alex:勤俭的,节约的。)

OK, so that's it for today's class. Thank you so much for listening.

—So, Alex, you wanna go get some drinks?
—OK, sure, but remember it's your turn to pay.
—Oh...uh. I forgot... Actually my cats are waiting at home for me, so I can't make it today.
—You are so cheap.

Day 54

"睡觉"除了用 *sleep* 表示，
还可以用什么表达更地道？

D: Man, even though we're 30, we look and feel so young.

A: Ya, man, we are so youthful.

D: Totally, I have so much energy.

A: Me too. Forever young.

D: So… it's 9 p.m. now. I'd better **hit the sack**.

A: It's 9 p.m.? Really? Way passed my bed time.

D: Good night, man.

A: Good night.

听完今天的对话之后，我们要来学习一个你每天都能用到的口语表达。

Oh, I'm so tired. I think I'm gonna hit the sack. "**Hit the sack**" means "*go to bed*". Where does this come from?

Actually farmers used to be quite poor, and they didn't have beds, but they would have a sack and they would fill the sack with something soft, maybe hay, and then they would just lie on the sack and go to sleep. So we say hit the sack. It means go to bed.

"hit the sack" 这个表达特别有意思，原本指一些农民在麻袋（sack 的意思是"麻袋"）里塞一些干草，这样睡觉比较暖和，躺上去也比较软。后来这个表达流传下来，hit the sack 就相当于 go to bed。

OK, so the bonus for today is a very very similar expression. We said hit the sack. Maybe if you had a sack, you would fill it with hay, and then it would be very comfortable.

Some farmers wouldn't even have a sack. They would just sleep on the hay, so we say hit the hay. **Hit the hay** also means **go to bed**.

因为 hay 就是"干草"的意思！（大白：涨知识！）

美国年轻人口中的 MIA 是什么意思？

D: Man, I'm so worried about Jason. He's been **MIA** for 3 days.

A: I'm sure he's okay.

D: Let's go to his apartment and check on him.

A: Dude, I'm sure he's fine.

D: No, I'm really worried about him. I care about him. We need to go check on him now!

A: But Sally invited us to her party, you know?

D: Really…? Let's go, bro!

A: What about Jason?

D: Who's Jason? It's party time!

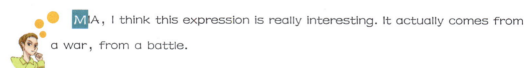

OK, 听完今天的对话之后，我们要学习一个非常地道的表达，叫"MIA"。

MIA, I think this expression is really interesting. It actually comes from a war, from a battle.

If somebody was safe, they would be listed as being safe. People know where they are.

If somebody was killed, they would be listed as KIA, killed in action.

But if nobody knew where they were, maybe they were killed, maybe they were captured by the enemy, maybe they are safe, but no one knows.

They would be **MIA**. It means **missing in action**.

So now when we say missing in action, **MIA**, it means **we don't know where someone is**.

MIA,"missing in action",本来指打仗的时候不知道士兵去哪儿了,不知去向,不知死活,就消失了,叫"missing in action"。现在用来指某个人消失了。

OK, so for today's bonus. We mentioned **KIA** which means **killed in action**. We don't actually use this in everyday English, but what we do say is, for example, if I haven't seen Alex in a few days, I might ask somebody "**Is Alex still alive**?" It means **where's Alex**?

I know he's still alive, but it's just a popular expression that we use.

今天实际有两个 bonus,第一个是 KIA,指的是"killed in action"。但这个表达在生活中不怎么能用到。

经常用到的,比如说你跟你朋友很久没见了,你问另外一个朋友:"Is Darby still alive?"(他还活着的吧?)或者是你给朋友发微信:"Are you still alive?"(你还活着吧?)意思是好久没有你的信儿了。

Day 56

"怀恨在心"用英语怎么说？

D: Hey, man, you need to stop **holding a grudge** against Jason.
A: I don't have a grudge. I let it go long ago.
D: Are you sure? He bullied you a lot in high school.
A: Whatever. I let it go. That was so many years ago.
D: Oh, OK, that's good. Because he's coming to the party tonight…
A: What? I'm gonna kick his ass! I hate him!

听完今天的对话之后，我们要学习一个非常地道的表达，叫"hold a grudge"。

Ya, you can hold a grudge against someone, or actually against something. For example, if somebody hurt you a long time ago, and you're still angry about it, that's called holding a grudge.

Usually if **you stay angry about something and you can't let it go for too long**, we say to **hold a grudge**.

You can also hold a grudge against, for example, a company. If you get fired, you can be really angry. Starbucks fired me. I hate them. I hold a grudge against (it).

OK, hold a grudge 就是"记仇"。就像在对话当中,Jason 在上学的时候经常欺负我,所以,I hold a grudge against Jason. (我记他的仇。)

All right. So it's time for today's bonus. If somebody is holding a grudge for too long against other company or their boss, we'll say **let it go**. (Singing:Let it go... let it go...) It means maybe "放下"。

"Let it go."译为"放下"。当别人一直因某事耿耿于怀的时候,或者因为什么事情放不下的时候,你就可以用英文说 let it go,就这样吧,让 ta 随风而去吧。

"酒肉朋友"用英语怎么说？

A: Hey, man, wanna hang out tonight?
D: Sure, bro. Let's go to the bar!
A: Cool. Oh, just to let you know I forgot my wallet. So…do you mind paying tonight?
D: Oh… Uh. I just remembered I have a date tonight. So…
A: Darby, you're such a **fair weather friend!**
D: Oh, uh… my mom's calling me. **Gotta go**. Bye!

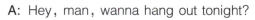

All right，听完今天的对话之后，我们要来学习一个非常有意思的表达，叫"fair weather friend"。

A fair weather friend **is** someone who's there for you, and they are your best friend, if you have money, if you're popular. But maybe you lose your money, you lose your popularity, and they disappear.

This is because fair weather means really nice weather. The sun's out. Everything is good. But if a storm comes, which means you lose your money, you are not so popular anymore. They disappear immediately.

Alex，allow me to 炫耀我的中文，fair weather friend 就是指"酒肉朋友，狐朋狗友"。

OK，我们今天学习的这个表达叫 fair weather friend。就是指当你得势的时候，围在你身边夸你，跟你一起吃饭、喝酒，占你便宜的朋友。但是当你突然有一天失势了，你没有什么利用价值的时候，他们就立马消失了。这种朋友就叫 fair weather friend。

OK, so for today's bonus. A very local expression. **If you need to leave, you can say** gotta go or maybe **I gotta go**. You can also say **I gotta run**. So I gotta go. Bye!

在今天的 bonus 当中，我们学习了一个每天都会用到的非常地道的表达，叫 gotta go。当你要离开的时候可以跟对方说 gotta go。大白，还有其他的表达方式可以说吗？

对，uh, gotta run, I gotta run.

OK, that's it for today's class. Thank you so much for listening.

—Uh, boss, I'm gonna go home earlier today, so gotta go. Bye.
—You get back here!

Day 58

"左右为难"用英语怎么说？

D: Hey, man, uh… I'm really confused right now.

A: What's wrong, bro?

D: It's just, I'm **on the fence**.

A: On the fence about what?

D: So many girls like me. How can I choose a girlfriend?

A: I hate you. I'm on the fence about whether I'm gonna punch you in the face.

D: No! Don't ruin my beautiful looks!

A: Bye.

OK, 听完今天的对话之后，我们要来学习一个非常地道的表达，叫 "**on the fence**"。真的只有 native speaker 才知道的一个表达哦！

Ya, so if you imagine you're standing on a fence, you can choose to jump off one side, or you can choose to jump off the other side. So if you are **on the fence**, it means **you have options, but you haven't decided which one to choose**.

For example, I could say, I'm on the fence about what I'm gonna have for dinner. I could have hot pot. I could have Chongqing noodles. So many delicious choices. So I'm on the fence.

在中文中，可以把这个表达翻译成左右为难，就是不知道该怎么做选择。

比如很多女孩，当选择衣服的时候，觉得这件也好看，那件也好看，每件都想要！这个时候就可以说"I'm on the fence."，即"好难选"。

OK, so it's time for today's bonus. I'm gonna teach you two words. **Decisive**, means **a person who is really able to make decisions very very quickly**. (Alex：果断的。)（That's) a decisive person.

An **indecisive** person,（Alex：优柔寡断的，就是做决定特别特别难。）**always on the fence**, can't decide.

—Hey, boss, so many girls like me. How can I choose a girlfriend?
—You're such a liar. Nobody likes you.
—Aw.
—Bye！

Day 59

同样表示"再见", see you soon 和 see you later 有什么区别呢？

D: Hey, Alex. I'm not feeling so good. Is it OK if I go home for a bit?

A: Oh, all right.

D: Thanks, I'll come back in the afternoon. **See you soon.**

A: Actually you can have a rest. No need to come back if you are sick.

D: Oh, OK, thank you! You are such a nice boss! I guess I'll **see you later.**

A: See you later!

All right, 听完这个对话之后呢，我们今天来学习重要的两个表达：see you later 和 see you soon。为什么要讲这两个表达呢？很多同学都觉得这两个表达不是一样的吗？甚至很多英语老师都不知道它们的区别。

So, Darby, what's the difference between "see you later" and "see you soon"?

OK, let's start with "see you later".

If I say to someone "see you later", it means I don't know exactly when I'll see them again. It could be tomorrow. It could be two days later. It could be a year later! (Alex: yeah.) I have no idea.

If I say "see you soon", it usually means we have a plan to meet, maybe within two hours, within three hour.

Maybe we have plan to meet at 3 p.m. to drink coffee, and it's 12 o'clock, (then we can say:) see you soon, see you at 3.

All right, 不知道大白的全英文解释大家有没有听懂呢？

see you later 的意思就是，在说了再见之后不知道什么具体的时候能再次见面，这个时候我们就用 see you later。

那什么时候用 see you soon 呢？ 就是当我们在说再见的时候定了一个时间，相对较短，比如"2个小时之后我们一起喝咖啡"，或者是"今天晚上一起吃晚餐"，就可以说 see you soon。

在今天的对话当中，大白说他生病了，但他下午还要回来，这时他说再见用的是 see you soon，后来我说如果你生病的话就不用回来，因为他也不知道什么时候（身体）能好，所以不知道什么时候能再见，这时他就用了 see you later。

Now as a bonus, we have "**hope to see you soon**". It actually means the same as "see you later", because we don't have a fixed time when we're gonna meet them. It could be tomorrow. It could be a month from now. It could be a year from now.

But **it sounds a lot more warm because we're saying** "**hope**".

我们今天给大家带来的 bonus 是 hope to see you soon。就像大白说的，hope to see you soon 表达的意思其实跟 see you later 是一样的，不知道什么时候能见面，但是当你说出这句话的时候，对方就会觉得特别温暖。因为这表达了你特别想很快地再见到他。Hope to see you soon！

Day 60

原来 *salty* 在口语中除了表示"咸的",还可以表示这个意思。

D: Hey, man, my last video got 1 million likes. Yours got 100! Hahaha!
A: Shut up! It's only because I wrote your script!
D: Don't be so **salty**. Obviously it's because I'm handsome.
A: Ya, but I noticed you're starting to get wrinkles.
D: Oh, my God. Really? My life is over!

OK,听完今天的对话之后,我们要来学习一个特别地道的表达,叫"salty"。salty 的原意指的是什么东西"很咸",那在今天的对话当中 salty 是什么意思呢?

I really really love this expression. It's brand new! "**Salty**", we used to say "bitter". It means **you can't get over something, you are a "sore loser"**.

For example, if Alex and I played like ping pong, and Alex beat me, and I said, "It's because I was feeling sick. It's because I injured my hand." And Alex said, "No, you're just being salty." It means that I'm crying about something and I can't get over it.

We say salty because when you cry, your tears are salty. So you could say, "Quit crying about it. Don't be so salty."

salty 这个词现在真的非常流行,它<u>一般用于比赛当中或者竞赛当中</u>。

我举两个例子。第一个例子是大白刚才说的,比如我们俩打乒乓球,我把他打败了以后,他就在那儿找各种原因:哎呀我的手受伤了,

我这边的阳光刺眼了……我就会说:"Don't be so salty."

或者在职场当中,比如说你们公司某一个长得漂亮的同事升职了,这个时候其他(某些)同事就说:哎呀,还不是因为她跟老板关系好!这种行为就是"being salty"。你就可以对他们说:"Don't be so salty"

OK,so it's time for today's bonus. Salty is an adjective, but if you wanna use a noun, you could say, "Don't be such a sore loser."

A sore loser is somebody who after losing a competition, makes a bunch of excuses. Maybe they insult the opponent that beat them. We say they're being such a sore loser.

今天的 bonus 当中,大白教了大家一个表达叫"sore loser"。sore 就是"酸的",比如说你的肌肉比较"酸",还有就是表示嗓子疼常用的是 sore。sore loser 这个表达一般用来形容那些在比赛当中输了但是输不起而找各种理由的人。

—Hey, Alex, let's go running.
—All right! Let's go!
—All right!
—Are you ready? 3, 2, 1, go!
—Darby, can you run faster? I'm waiting for you!
—It's only because my shoes are too small! It hurts my feet.
—Don't be so salty! Bye!

Day 61

安慰别人最强有力的一句英文是什么？

D: Hey, man, I'm so sad.
A: What's wrong dude?
D: My girlfriend dumped me.
A: Aw, man, don't worry. It's not the end of the world.
D: Ya, but she said she dumped me because I'm a loser with no job.
A: Hmm… maybe it is the end of the world for you.

听完今天的对话之后，我们要来学习一个非常重要的表达，这句话你可能每天都会用到：It's not the end of the world.

Yeah, I recommend everyone remembers this sentence: It's not the end of the world. We use this all the time to console or to comfort someone, if they feel bad.

Maybe my girlfriend breaks up with me, and I feel like my world is falling apart. Alex can say, "It's not the end of the world." It means tomorrow will still happen. You need to "加油". You need to keep going. Everything will be OK.

OK，"**It's not the end of the world**." 是用来安抚朋友的常用表达。

比如说大白的女朋友跟他分手了，我就说："Come on, man, it's not the end of the world. There're so many fish in the sea." Right? 就是"天涯何处无芳草"的意思。

如果你的朋友不开心了，你就告诉 ta："It's not the end of the world." 又不是世界末日，明天还会来的。

OK, for the bonus. You can say that someone breaks up with you. My girlfriend broke up with me. But a more local way of saying it is "to **get dumped**". My girlfriend dumped me.（被甩了。）

—Yeah, "dump" 是 "甩" 的意思.

—So sad.

—Yeah, that's you.

—No way. man. Lots of girls like me.

—Then, why don't you have a girlfriend?

Day 62

parking ticket

不是"停车票"哦！

A: Man, you got a parking ticket. That sucks!

D: Ya, whatever.

A: But that's expensive, right?

D: No worries. It's just **a drop in the bucket** for me. I'm rich, bro.

A: Then why are you wearing shoes that cost 50 RMB?

D: Uh…

OK，今天我们要学习一个非常有趣的表达叫"drop in the bucket"。

Yeah, "a drop in the bucket", it means a really really really small amount that doesn't matter. If you picture a really big bucket filled with water, and then a drop of water falls into that bucket, **it doesn't mean anything**. (Alex: It's nothing.)

So, we usually use this, for example, if a really really rich person gets fined like 100 RMB, for them it's nothing. It's just a drop in the bucket. Alex, allow me to 炫耀我的中文：九牛一毛.

"drop in the bucket",就像大白说的,是"九牛一毛"的意思。"drop"是"水滴",然后"bucket"是"水桶"。你想象一下:一滴水对于一大桶水来说,它真的是九牛一毛。

这个短语可以用来形容那些有钱人,比如说 ta 被罚款,罚了 100 块钱,可对于 ta 来说这点儿罚款就是九牛一毛。That's just a drop in the bucket.

OK,so for today's bonus. In English we say "a **parking ticket**", it doesn't mean the ticket you get to park in a parking lot. A parking ticket means **you've parked in the wrong place, and you get a ticket, and you get fined a certain amount of money that you have to pay as a penalty**.

OK,今天的这个 bonus,很多同学都会误解它的意思。"**parking ticket**",它不是指"停车票",而是指"罚单",就是你停车停到了不该停的地方,被交警贴了一张罚单,那个"罚单"就叫"parking ticket"。

We could also say "speeding ticket"。"speeding ticket" 因为 speed 是"速度"的意思,就是说你开车超速了,那么 speeding ticket 就是"超速罚单"的意思。

Day 63

喜欢喝酒的朋友们一定要知道的英文单词！

D: Hey, man, did you party last night?

A: Ya, I went to an awesome party.

D: Don't drink too much **booze**. It can make you fat. It's bad for your health.

D: Wow, thanks for your advice, and thanks for truly caring about me.

A: No, I mean if you get fat, we'll lose fans and I won't make as much money.

D: I hate you.

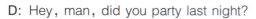

听完今天的对话之后，我们要来学习一个很有趣的表达，叫 "booze"。

Ya, **booze is just another word for alcohol**. So it can actually mean... it can mean anything. It can mean beer, it can mean wine（Alex：Whiskey.），it can mean vodka, and any type of alcohol we can call "booze".

And we can also use this word as a verb, not just a noun. We can say, for example, "I was out boozing last night. All night I was boozing."

OK, booze 这个词在口语当中经常可以用到，指的是 "酒"，各种各样的酒都可以叫 booze。就像大白说的，它除了当名词用之外，还可以做动词，booze 也可以指 "喝酒"。

OK, so for today's bonus, if you're out boozing, perhaps at a bar, and you want to "搭讪", go talk to someone, it's OK in English. In western countries it's OK to go up to someone and say, "Can I buy you a drink?" "May I buy you a drink?" Maybe in China you don't do this? We say "可以一起喝一杯吗？" 或者是 "我能要你的微信吗？"

So if someone comes to you and wants to buy you a drink, you have two options. If 他长得好帅，帅死了, you can say, "**Wow, thanks! That's so kind of you.**" That's a polite way of saying it. If 他丑死了, you can say, "**I'm waiting for my boyfriend.**"

在西方国家的酒吧文化里，如果你要去搭讪，一般都会说："Can I buy you a drink?" 我可以给你买一杯喝的吗？如果对方同意的话，基本上就可以开始对话了，可以相互了解，聊一聊，喝一杯（drink）。如果你要拒绝对方，就可以说："I'm waiting for my boyfriend."

My muscular, strong, body-building boyfriend!

—Hey, Alex. Can I buy you a drink?

—No, thank you. Bye!

Day 64

"摇钱树"用英语怎么说？

D: Boss, sometimes I feel like I'm just your **cash cow**.
A: No way, man. We're friends. I care about you.
D: Anyways, I'm going to Vancouver. So I'll be back next week.
A: I really hope you have a safe flight, man.
D: Oh, thanks. I appreciate that.
A: Of course I hope the flight is safe. If you die, I'll lose money.
D: You're a terrible person!

OK，我相信你们一定非常喜欢这个对话。今天要学习一个很有趣的表达叫"cash cow"。

Yeah, this is actually really easy to explain. If you're farmer, you raise a cow (奶牛), and you feed it, and you invest money into it, and you make sure that it grows to be strong and big, and then you sell it for a bunch of money. So, allow me to 炫耀我的中文：摇钱树.

Yeah, **cash cow** 就是"摇钱树"的意思。

OK, for today's bonus. Another word for cash or money is "**bread**". (Alex: bread?) Yeah, bread, and we have an expression called "**breadwinner**".

The breadwinner **is the person in a family who makes the money**, so traditionally it would be like the man, that would be the breadwinner in the family. But now, a lot of the time, women, the wives are the breadwinners. They make more money than men. So either one can be the breadwinner.

　　在今天的 bonus 当中，我们学习了一个表达叫：breadwinner。实际上有很多 rapper，就是那种唱 hip-pop 音乐的，他们把 bread 当成 cash。breadwinner 指的是 "一家的经济支柱"。很多时候大家会觉得好像男人才能做这个 breadwinner，但实际上现在在很多家庭里面，女生也可以做 breadwinner。

　　—Darby, who is the breadwinner in you family?
　　—Uh…I don't have a family. 我是单身狗。
　　—OK, bye.
　　—Bye.

Day 65

怎样用英文鼓励你的朋友去表白？

D: Man, you've been obsessed with that girl for like 2 years.
A: I know. I can't help it.
D: But you never ever tell her. You need to **grab life by the horns**, man. Just do it!
A: Man, you're right. I need to quit waiting! I'm gonna go over there and tell her I love her.
D: So, how'd it go?
A: Wow. Um… she's not **into** guys.
D: Oh, well, that's too bad.

All right，听完今天的对话之后，我们要来学习一个非常地道的表达，这个表达可以用来去鼓励你身边的朋友。

Yeah, we say "to **grab life by the horns**", or we'll often tell somebody "You need to grab life by the horns". It means **don't wait, it means don't delay, you need to control your own life**. So don't be shy, be confident! and grab life by the horns. Do what you want to do.

So where does this expression come from? It comes from bull riding, which is a very dangerous activity. If you do bull riding, you need to stay on top of a bull（公牛）, and you need to hold its horns, but you need to be very brave to be able to do this.

今天这个表达"to grab life by the horns"来自于斗牛比赛。当斗牛士骑上牛之后，需要用手抓住牛的角，所以就衍生出了这个表达。因为抓住牛角就是为了控制住牛。to grab life by the horns，就是抓住生活的"角"，成为生活的主宰。

OK, so for today's bonus, you heard Alex say that the girl is not **into** guys. OK, **to be "into" something means to like it.** I'm really into football, for example. It means I really like football.

But we also use this to express whether somebody likes guys or girls. So if a guy is into girls, it means he's"直男"。He's straight.

今天的 bonus 部分我们学习了一个表达，be into something 或者 be into someone。

I'm really into coffee. 我特别喜欢咖啡。I'm really into that girl. 我特别喜欢那个女孩。

—Alex, are you into girls or guys?
—Girls, for sure.
—Me too!
—Bye!

表达"酗酒""煲剧"用这个词更地道！

D: Man, you're always **binge**-playing video games.
A: I know, man. I'm just a gamer. I love it.
D: You need to get out of the house more.
A: Ya, maybe you're right. What do you do for fun?
D: I go out and drink beer every night.
A: You binge-drink? Isn't that worse for your health than binge-gaming?
D: Uh... actually I think it's cool that you play games. Keep it up, man!
A: You idiot.

听完今天的对话之后，我们要来学习一个现在非常流行的表达，叫"binge"，就是"煲……"。

"Binge", we use this all the time. It's very popular right now. Actually it comes from drinking **too much**. "Binge-drinking" means to drink way too much, **excessively**, maybe "酗酒".

But we can use binge with many other words. You can put it with playing video games. Binge-playing video games means to play too many video games, like 10 hours in a row. My mom binge-watches TV shows, 6 episodes in a row!

In other words, Allow me to 炫耀我的中文：煲剧!

我们今天学习的这个表达与"喝酒"有关，当形容没有节制地喝酒时，我们称之为"酗酒"，英文叫 binge-drinking。后来多用于形容那些追剧的情形，天天看剧，一天看十几集电视剧，这种情况就可以叫"煲剧"，binge-watching TV series。

All right, so for today's bonus, we're gonna give you another example of binging. You can binge-eat. Sometimes in movie you'll see a girl and her boyfriend break up, and she's really really sad, and she takes a bunch of ice cream, and eats and eats and eats, to comfort herself. We can call this **binge-eating**.

今天的 bonus 部分讲了一个词叫 binge-eat。如果想形容某人暴饮暴食就可以说他"binge-eating"。

—So Alex, what do you binge on?
—Speak like a native! That's our own show.
—Get over yourself!
—Bye.

Day 67

"扣篮"的英文居然还可以这么用？

D: Man, my broadcast class last night was a **slam dunk**!

A: Oh, really? Why do you think so?

D: The students love me, bro. Must be my charm. I'm the best teacher.

A: Umm... then why did you get a 3-star review?

D: What?

A: One comment is "The teacher isn't very handsome."

D: What? I quit! I'm never teaching again!

A: Hahaha!

我们今天要学习的这个表达看过NBA的同学应该都知道，"slam dunk"，就是"扣篮"。

A **slam dunk** is when a guy jumps in the air and slams the basketball into the hoop. And this is good, right?

Ya, awesome.

Ya it's a success. So we can use this in everyday life. If something is **successful**, we can call it a "slam dunk". I can say my broadcast class last night, it was so good, and it was a slam dunk. It means it was **awesome**.

It was **wonderful**.

　　　　slam dunk 这个表达来自于篮球比赛（中的）扣篮，当我们想要说什么东西很棒的时候，就可以用这个短语，也可以（用它来）比喻我们生活中取得的一些成功。For example, our course, "我们天天练"的课程, totally a slam dunk, 超棒超赞超牛。

———————— ○ ————————

OK, so for today's bonus, you heard me say in the conversation "**must be my charm**". The students love me. Must be my charm. Charm comes form charming. If a person is charming，allow me to 炫耀我的中文：特别有魅力.

　　"Must be my charm." 我们在口语当中也可以经常用到这个表达。为什么这么多人喜欢我们的课程呢？Must be my charm.（Darby：对！）

　　—So Alex, why do you think so many people like us?
　　—Must be our charm.
　　—Bye.

Day 68

"容易上当受骗的"用英语怎么说？

D: Hey, Alex, I totally have a new girlfriend.
A: What? Again?
D: We've been talking on the Internet. She says she loves me. She's gonna come visit me.
A: Um... really? Are you sure she loves you?
D: Obviously. She told me! So I sent her 2,000 yuan to take a plane here.
A: What? You sent her money?
D: Ya. Can't wait till she gets here.
A: You are such a **gullible** idiot. She's not coming.
D: It's true love, okay? She'll be here!

听完今天的对话之后，我们要来学习一个非常高级的单词，但是在生活当中也经常会遇到，叫"gullible"。

Yeah, **gullible**, we use this word all the time. Actually I find that most Chinese people actually don't know this word, so it's a new word, and it's an adjective.

If you are gullible, it means **you believe people too easily**, so it's very easy for people to cheat you. Like in the conversation, this girl on the Internet said, "Oh, I love you. Send me some money." I believed that she loved me, and I sent her some money. Ugh, so gullible, so easily cheated.

我们今天学习的这个词"gullible",它可以形容那些我们身边经常上当受骗、特别容易相信别人的这类人,very gullible。

OK, for today's bonus, we're gonna teach you a new word. The word is "**scam**". A scam is **to cheat somebody**. For example, in the conversation, this person maybe pretending to be a girl, pretending to fall in love with someone online, and then asking for money. We could say this is a scam.

OK,在今天的 bonus 中,我们学习的这个词叫"scam"。作为动词它可以用作 to scam somebody,就是去欺诈某人。那它同时也可以作为一个名词,叫作"骗局"。

—Hey, Alex, you know I have a new girlfriend.

—What? Again?

—Yeah, she's so kind. She sells tea because her grandpa is in the hospital.

—How much did you spend on that?

—Only like 1,500 RMB.

—You're such a gullible idiot.

—It's true love, OK?

—Bye!

Day 69

如何用 interesting 表达"呵呵"的意思？

D: Man, I've finally found true love.
A: Really?
D: I met a girl on the bus. She wanted my number.
A: Wow. Good for you!
D: Ya, and now she's selling me insurance.
A: What? You're paying her?
D: Of course. She's selling me insurance because she cares so much about me!
A: Em, **interesting**… you are such a gullible idiot.
D: What?

All right，我们学习的这个词其实大家都认识，叫作 "interesting" 就是"有趣的"意思。"Oh, that's very interesting."（真有趣）。同时，在北美有些人为表达特别夸张的情感会读作 "inter-resting"。在今天的对话当中，"interesting" 就不是我们平时常用的那个意思。

In English, it's really important to know the way that you say a word.

For example, you can say, "Wow, interesting!" It means you really are interested.（非常有趣）But if you say, "**Em, interesting**." This kind of have a sarcastic meaning. Allow me to 炫耀我的中文：呵呵.

—Emm, interesting.
—Interesting.

All right, for today's bonus, we have a very simple fixed expression. You heard Alex say to me "**good for you**". It just means "**you did a good job**", and I'm happy for you. It's like a compliment.

For example, my friend could say, "I got a promotion at work." I could say, "Oh, good for you, man." Or they could say, "I got a new job, a really good job." Good for you.

"good for you" 这个短语在生活当中每天都可以用到，翻译成中文可以是"真有你的"。当你听到对方的好消息的时候，你就可以说："Good for you."

—Hey, Alex, I have a new girlfriend.
—Em, interesting.

Day 70

自信的人必备的一句英文！

A: Hey, man, let's start recording our course.
D: Great. Sounds good.
A: This conversation is a little difficult. Are you ready?
D: Bro, don't worry. **I was born ready!**
A: OK, what's your first line?
D: Um... hold on, let me check the script.
A: You idiot.

OK，听完今天的对话之后，我们要来学习一个非常地道的表达：I was born ready.

I was born ready. This is a super confident way of saying that you are prepared, and you are ready to do something. It means **in your whole life, you've been ready for this, and it's gonna be really really easy.**

You could say, "Are you ready to record the course?" "I was born ready!" It means of course I'm ready.

I was born ready. 这句话特别能够体现你的信心，就是当对方问你："你准备好了吗？ Are you ready？" 你就可以说：I was born ready. 你在参加一些选秀节目或者你看选秀节目的时候，经常听到裁判会问：Are you ready？ 然后你或者选手就可以说：I was born ready. "我从生下来那一刻就准备好了。"

OK, for the bonus today, we're gonna teach you another expression that uses born. **I wasn't born yesterday**. We use this if somebody tell us something that's very obvious, and we say, "I'm not stupid. I wasn't born yesterday. I know. OK?"

"I wasn't born yesterday." 就是"我又不是三岁小孩"的意思。当对方跟你讲一些显而易见的事情的时候，你就可以怼对方说：I wasn't born yesterday. 我又不是昨天才出生的，我又不是三岁小孩儿，我知道！

Day 71

boss 居然还可以这么用！

D: Boss, my class last night was awesome.
A: That's great.
D: Ya. The students love me.
A: You're such a good teacher.
D: I taught that class **like a boss**! So confident.
A: That's good to know!
D: So, how about a raise?
A: Shut up!
D: Aw…

OK，听完今天的对话之后，我们要来学习一个非常有意思的表达叫"like a boss"。

Yeah, to do something like a boss. It's to do something really well, really confidently. This might be confusion for some people, because "a boss" is "老板", but "**like a boss**" means **to do something really really awesome with a lot of confidence**.

For example, if one of my friends goes and talks to a really beautiful girl and gets her number, I could say, "Wow, you did that like a boss."

OK，"do something like a boss" 就是形容当某人完成了一件事情，而且完成得特别好，ta 本人又表现得特别自信。这时你就可以说：You did that like a boss.

OK, for the bonus today, there's actually many ways to use the word "boss". "Boss" means "老板", right? You can say to do something like a boss, to do something really confidently.

But there's also an adj ectove, that's "**bossy**". If someone is bossy, it means they **try to control everyone around them**, and they **try to control everything**. So people don't like bossy people.

"do something like a boss" 是一个比较褒义的说法，而 "bossy" 相对来说却是一个比较贬义的词，形容某人喜欢控制别人，而且喜欢控制一切，就是做事情有点儿 over 的那种感觉。

—Hey, Alex, what do you think of my teaching style?
—You teach like a boss.
—Thanks, man!

形容一个人状态很好可以用 on fire 吗?

D: I'm the best, boss.
A: Why's that?
D: I just won 7 games of LOL.
A: Wow, really?
D: Ya, I am **on fire** right now!
A: That's nice, Darby, but guess what?
D: What?
A: No playing games at work. That's a 500-yuan fine.
D: Aw…

All right, 听完今天的对话之后，我们要来学习一个非常地道的表达叫"on fire"。

If you are **on fire**, it means you're **doing something really really well**.

Sometimes we use this in sports, for example, basketball. If Lebron James is having a really really good game, and every shot he's taking is going in, we could say, "Wow, he is on fire!"

Or if you are playing maybe a game, and you win 7 in a row, and you are playing so well, (you can say) "Wow, I am on fire!"

"I am on fire." 这个表达我们每天都可以用到。当你**做某件事情状态非常好**的时候，你就可以说"I'm on fire."。当夸赞对方状态特别好的时候，你就可以说"You are on fire."

OK, so for today's bonus. Everybody knows the word "**fine**". "I'm fine, thank you. And you?" But here it has another meaning. Allow me to 炫耀我的中文：罚款.

In the conversation it's used as a noun. So you can say, "I got a 100-yuan fine." "I got a 500-yuan fine." But you can also use it as a verb, to fine somebody. e.g. My boss fined me.

OK, fine 在今天的对话中作为名词是"罚款"的意思。同时它也可以作为动词使用，to fine somebody 就是"罚某人的款"的意思。如果说"我被罚款了"，就可以说："I got fined."

—Hey, boss, I've practicing this new Chinese song for the last two hours. Do you wanna hear?
—Darby, no singing song at work. That's 100-yuan fine.
—Aw.

Day 73

shut up 除了表示"闭嘴"，还有这个意思！

A: Darby, you look good today.

D: Really? You mean it?

A: Ya, really handsome. Nice outfit.

D: Wow, thanks, boss.

A: You're a good-looking guy.

D: **Shut up**! You're just saying that to make me feel good.

A: Mm... ya, actually you're right. You're just average.

D: I hate you so much right now.

OK, 听完今天的对话之后，我们要来学习"shut up"除了表示"闭嘴"之外的表达。

Yeah, most Chinese people know "shut up". It means "闭嘴". It's kind of a mean thing to say to someone. (Alex: Very rude.) Yeah, it's rude.

But there's another way of saying "shut up". Of course, "语气" is very important. The way that you say a word is really important.

If someone compliments you, "Oh, you are so handsome today!" And you say "Shut up". It means the same as "哪里哪里".

And another way of using "shut up" is, in **a romantic way**, say there is a couple, and the man says to the woman "I love you", and the woman says "I love you more". The man says "Shut up! I love you more." The woman says "Shut up! I love you more."

Shut up, Darby! Haha!

另外一种情境是用于夫妇（couple）之间，两个人相互说（更）爱对方，不停地说"Shut up! I love you more."。太肉麻了好吗！

All right, so for today's bonus, you heard Alex say to me I'm just **average**. It means "**just OK, just all right, nothing special**". Maybe in Chinese you will say "一般般".

—Yeah, right, 长相平平.
—Yeah, but obviously I'm not just average. I'm a perfect 10. I'm super handsome!
—Shut up!
—Hey, Alex, you don't think I'm a ten?
—You are just five. Shut up!
—You shut up!

Day 74

"筋疲力尽"用英语怎么说？

A: Hey, where are you?
D: Boss, I can't come to work today.
A: Why's that?
D: I'm just **burnt out**. So much work lately.
A: Oh, well, then you can stay home.
D: Thanks so much. I appreciate it.
A: But you forgot, today's the company party. Lots of beer.
D: ...I'll be there in ten

OK, 听完今天的对话之后，我们要来学习一个非常有趣的表达叫"burnt out"。

Yeah, we use this expression a lot, especially when it comes to work. If you work really really hard, and you work hard every day, you can get **burnt out**. It means **you lose enthusiasm for your job, You feel tired, You need a rest.**

And we can also use this, for example, for sports, because the NBA season is very long, right? 82 games. Maybe an athlete, maybe a basketball player, after 60 games, you'll feel really burnt out. They need a rest.

OK，burnt out，在中文当中其实有一个特别好的对应的词叫"筋疲力尽"，指你已经累到不行了。如果是在工作的话，你就没有办法再继续工作了，因为你已经burnt out了。如果一个运动员累到无法继续运动了，就叫burnt out。

OK, for today's bonus. You heard me say "**I'll be there in ten.**" The full sentence should be：**I'll be there in ten minutes.**

But in English we like to shorten things and make it easier for us to say, so we can just say, "I'll be there in ten." Everybody knows that it means ten minutes. You can also just say, "Be there in ten."

对话的最后一句话：**I'll be there in ten.** 这句话完整的句子是：**I'll be there in ten minutes.**

Native speaker 为了节约时间，为了简便，说成了"I'll be there in ten."。ten 后面其实少了"分钟"这个词，不过人们也能理解。那更简短的是什么呢？Be there in ten.

—Hey, Alex, I've been working so hard. I'm really burnt out. I'm just gonna go home and sleep, OK?
—Um...All right, but...Emily's having a party tonight.
—I'll be there.
—Bye.

Day 75

如何用英语表达"兄弟情义"?

A: Hey, man, I know we make fun of each other a lot, but you're a good friend.

D: Aw, thanks, man. You're a good friend too.

A: I'm lucky to have met you.

D: I feel the same way.

A: Let's hug it out. This is a real **bromance**!

D: Ya, gimme a hug. Love you, man!

A: Love you too.

D: Um, I feel like that was a little awkward.

A: Ya... I think I'll go see my girlfriend.

D: Ya... uh, me too. I totally love girls.

A: Bye.

OK,我们今天要来学习一个特别有意思的组合词叫"bromance"。

A bromance, this is a really popular word right now. If two guys are really really good friends, we can say they're in a bromance.

It comes from the word "brother" which can mean friend, and the word "romance", and we put it together. It becomes "bromance".

bromance 是由"brother"加上"romance"组成的一个新词，用于形容两个男生之间，或者多个男生之间的这种兄弟情谊。Hey, Darby, do you have a word for girls?

Actually, there's no specific word for girls, because it's normal for girls to be good friends. You could say maybe they're "**besties**".

Oh, but this could be the bonus. There's a really interesting word that we usually use for girls. It can be used for guys too, but usually for girls.

It's "**frenemies**", we take the word "friend" and the word "enemy", and put them together. It means **girls who act like they're best friends when they're with each other, but then one of them leaves, they say some bad things about them.**

For example, two girls, one can say, "You're so cute today. I love your outfit. You look so good." And then the girl leaves, "She's so ugly."

OK, friend and enemy, 意思就是"当面是朋友，背地讲坏话"，组合成一个新的词叫作"**frenemy**"。

Day 76

"耙耳朵"用英语怎么说？

D: Hey, come hang out with the crew!

A: I can't tonight. My wife won't let me.

D: What? You're so **whipped**!

A: I'm not whipped. I just promised I'd have dinner with her.

D: Fine. Then let's chill tomorrow?

A: I can't.

D: why?

A: My wife is making me go to a romantic comedy with her.

D: You're so whipped. You're your wife's slave!

OK，听完今天的对话之后，我们要学习一个特别有意思的表达叫"**whipped**"。

Yeah, I love this expression and I use it a lot, because I'm at the age where my friends are starting to get married or they have girlfriends. We say "**whipped**", it means... Can I 炫耀我的重庆话？(Alex: OK.) "耙耳朵."

Because a whip is... How to say "whip" in Chinese? (Alex: 鞭子。) So a slave owner will use a whip to hit a slave, right? So if we say **someone is whipped**, it means **they're the slave of their wife or girlfriend**.

刚才大白在讲解的过程当中用了一个重庆话的地道表达："耙耳朵。"，(这个词)其实(是用来)形容那些怕老婆的人：You're so whipped. 每次他约我我都去不了，因为我跟我老婆有事儿。 他便说：You're so whipped.

whip 作为动词的时候，是指拿皮鞭去抽别人。"You're so whipped."就是"你被严格地管控、控制住了"的意思。

OK, for today's bonus. **Sometimes you don't even have to say "You're so whipped." Sometimes we just make the sound of a whip**. If I invite Alex out for dinner, and he says, "Oh, my wife won't let me. I can't go."（大白模仿鞭子声）

—Hey, Alex, you wanna go get some beer?
—Oh, sorry, my wife won't let me.

hook up 有这么多意思，你知道吗？

A: Darby, your acting is terrible.

D: I'm trying my best, okay?

A: You need to get better. If you don't improve, we'll lose fans.

D: Okay, sure. **Hook me up with** an acting trainer.

A: Okay. Good idea.

D: Cool. It's 500 RMB per hour. You can pay.

A: Um... actually, you know your acting is not that bad.

D: You're so cheap!

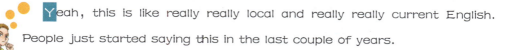

OK, 听完今天的对话之后，我们要学习一个特别有意思的表达叫 "hook me up with"。

Yeah, this is like really really local and really really current English. People just started saying this in the last couple of years.

"**Hook me up with something**" means **get me in contact with maybe something or someone**. So if I say "hook me up with an acting trainer", it means "find an acting trainer for me".

You can also say, for example, if you really like a girl, and you know their friend, you can tell their friend, "Hook me up with that girl." It means let me get in contact with that girl.

"hook"的原意指的是"钩子",hook me up with 就是把两个人连接起来(联系起来)。大白说,"**Hook me up with an acting trainer.**"就是**帮我找一个表演老师**。如果你想认识某人,"hook me up with"就是"帮我介绍一下某人"的意思。

OK, for today's bonus. You just learned "hook me up with", but you can also say "hook up with". You can hook up with someone. For example, I could say, "**Let's hook up this afternoon and drink coffee.**" It means "**Let's hang out with each other.**"

—Alex, did you know "hook up" also has another meaning?
—Yeah, sure.
—If we said the guy and the girl hooked up last night, it means…(你懂的。)
—就是他们鬼混在一起了。
—对。
—他们能懂。

如何用英语表达"随大流"才够酷？

A: Man, what do you wanna do tonight?
D: Whatever. I'll just **go with the flow**.
A: Cool. Let's go eat hot pot.
D: Naw, man. It's too spicy.
A: Okay, how about we have some beers at that patio?
D: Naw, I don't feel like drinking.
A: So, what do you wanna do?
D: Whatever. I'll just **go with the flow**.
A: Oh, my God. You're so frustrating.

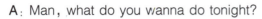

OK，听完今天的对话之后，我们要来学习一个非常酷的表达，叫"go with the flow"。

To go with the flow, it means just **do whatever other people wanna do**. If Alex says, "Hey, what do you wanna do tonight?" I say, "I'll just **go with the flow**." It means whatever he wants to do, I'll follow him. I'll do it with him.

"go with the flow"在中文当中有一个非常完美的翻译，叫"随大流"，即"听大家的"。"I'll go with the flow."

So just to explain where this expression comes from, a river has a flow, and it flows in a certain direction. If you just let yourself relax and flow with the river, it's all good. But if you try to swim against the flow, it's so hard.

OK, so for today's bonus, we will teach you a new word. Maybe you don't know it. "**Frustrating.**" **If someone or something is frustrating, it means it makes you angry, and it makes you annoyed.**

So if somebody is very indecisive, and they can't make up their mind, they can be very frustrating.

当某人快把你逼疯的时候，你快受不了了，你可以说，"You're so frustrating."

—Hey, Darby, what would you like for lunch?
—Whatever, man. Whatever you want. I'll go with the flow.
—Noodles?
—I'm on a diet, man. I'm not eating noodles.
—You're frustrating.

people person 原来是这个意思！

A: Hey, man, ready for the interview?
D: Of course. I'm a **people person**. They're gonna love me.
A: Wow. You're confident.
D: Everybody loves me. I'm great with people.
A: Then why do you spend every weekend at home alone?
D: Uh, because so many people invite me to parties, I just can't decide where to go.
A: Em, interesting.

OK, 听完今天的对话之后，我们要来学习一个稍微有点儿绕的地道表达 "people person"。

A people person is someone who's very outgoing, really likes people, but people also like them too. So we say they are people person. They're very very very extroverted.

For example, if somebody is always going to parties, always being invited to parties, always surrounded by many many friends, we can say, "Wow, he or she is a people person."

我们今天学到的这个 "people person" 指的是那种非常外向的人，很善于跟别人打交道的人，这样的人我们把 ta 叫作 "people person"。

OK, for today's bonus. A word that's kind of similar to "people person", and it's an adj ective. It's "**approachable**". You can say a person is approachable. It means that **people like to go and talk to them. People feel comfortable with them, and it's very easy to make friends with them**.

An approachable person usually looks very friendly. For example, my mom is very approachable.

She'll be waiting in line to buy something at a store, and someone will come and start telling her their life story. So she's very approachable.

"approachable" 翻译成中文是"面善的，看起来很友好的"的意思。当你觉得一个人很面善，自然就愿意去跟 ta 交往。

—So, Alex, are you approachable?
—Yeah, for sure. As long as they are hot.
—You're terrible person.
—No, I'm very approachable.
—Terrible person.

"塞翁失马,焉知非福"用英语怎么说?

D: Hey, man, when I quit my last job, I was really upset.
A: Really?
D: Ya. I felt depressed.
A: Ya. That sucks.
D: But because I felt depressed, I decided to make a douyin account to stay busy.
A: Right. And I discovered you and changed your life!
D: Ya. I guess being depressed was a blessing in disguise.
A: Happy to have you on my team, man!
D: Me too!
A&D: Aw.

OK,听完今天的对话之后,我们要来学习一个非常高级的表达,叫 "a blessing in disguise"。

"A blessing in disguise", we use this a lot. "A blessing" is a good thing. "In disguise" means it's pretending to be a bad thing.

So for example, we could say, you get fired from your job, and you think, "Oh, no, this is terrible." But, you go and you find a better job. You can say, "Wow, getting fired was actually a blessing in disguise."

Or another example, you get dumped by your girlfriend. You feel so depressed, you feel terrible, but you find a better girlfriend. Getting

dumped was a blessing in disguise.（Alex：你知道中文怎么说吗？）Allow me to 炫耀我的中文，"塞翁失马， 焉知非福。"（Alex：你真的有点儿厉害。）

OK, so it's time for today's bonus. We have another really good expression that uses blessing. We say "count your blessings".

If somebody feels depressed or sad, we can say, don't worry, count your blessings. It means think of all the good things in your life, and don't think of the bad things. You have a family, you have a home, you have a job, You have people who love you. These are blessings, so we say "count your blessings". **Don't think of the bad things. Count the good things.**

"Count your blessings."可以用来安慰你的朋友，当 ta 觉得很郁闷的时候，(可以对 ta 说) 想想你生活中好的事情，比如说：你想想你的家人和朋友，这些爱你的人。

—Hey, Alex, what do you think are the blessings in your life?

—I have a lot money.

—Shut up.

—Joking. I have a beautiful wife, and a cute daughter.

—Aw.

Day 81

如何用英语表达 "自己对做某事非常有信心"？

A: Hey, man, we're shooting important videos today.
D: No worries, man.
A: Did you bring your outfits?
D: Of course. I'm **on the ball** today. **You can count on me.**
A: OK, great. So you brought the scripts too then.
D: Oops. I forgot.
A: You're the worst.

OK, 听完今天的对话之后，我们来学习一个非常地道的表达，"on the ball"。

To be on the ball, it actually comes from football or soccer. If someone has the ball at their feet, it means they're in control of the game. So if you are **on the ball**, it means you are totally **in control of the situation.**

So for example, if I had a really really important video to shoot, and that day I bought a new outfit, I memorized my scripts so that I was prepared. I got my hair cut, so that I look good. You can say, wow, Darby is really on the ball today.

"on the ball" 一般用于你对局势完全能够把控，你非常自信你能做成某事的时候。比如我和大白在录课的时候，每次我们都可以说：We're on the ball.

OK，so for today's bonus, you heard me say "**You can count on me.**" This is a fixed expression that means **you can rely on me. I will support you. I'll be there for you**.

—Alex, do you mind if I sing?
—OK.
—You can count on me like one two three. I'll be there. It means you will be there for someone.
"You can count on me." 的意思就是 "**你可以信任我，你可以指望我**"。

For example, Alex allowed me to take control of this course, and write all of the scripts, because he can count on me.

—Ya, right, totally.
—And I can count on you…
—Shut up!

Day 82

"自我膨胀"用英语怎么表达？

A：Hey, man, just because you have fans now, don't get an **inflated ego**.
D：Come on. You know I'm a humble person.
A：Okay, good. I'm worried you'll start thinking you're better than other people.
D：No way, man. Everyone is equal. I'm just a normal guy.
A：Okay, good. So you wanna go to Jason's party on Saturday?
D：Jason? He only has 2,000 fans. He doesn't deserve to have me at his party.
A：Oh, God. It's starting to happen already.

OK，听完今天的对话之后，我们要来学习一个非常地道的表达叫"inflated ego"。

Yeah, an **inflated ego**, we usually use this, **if someone maybe started off not famous, not rich. But maybe became famous, became rich. They start thinking that they're maybe better than other people. They become a little bit arrogant.** We say this is an inflated ego. They have an inflated ego.

"Ego" means the way that you think about yourself. "Inflated" means to make something bigger. So we also sometimes say to have a big ego or inflated ego. If someone has an inflated ego, it means they think they're better than other people.

"inflated ego" 翻译成中文是"**自我膨胀**"的意思,有一些人取得一定成绩之后就开始膨胀,开始看不起人。

OK, for today's bonus. We are just gonna teach you this sentence: "**You deserve it**." This can be used in a good way or in a bad way.

For example, if my friend gets a really good job, because they worked very hard, I could say, "Good job, man. You deserve it."

Maybe if my friend drinks a bunch of beer, and then the next day, they feel a headache and they feel very sick, they feel hungover. We'll say, "Haha, you deserve it, man."

OK,今天的 bonus 部分我们讲的一句话叫:"**You deserve it**."这句话**可以用来夸奖一个人**,比如说 ta 努力工作,最后获得了年终奖,你就可以说:"You deserve it."(这是你应得的。)如果 ta 干了坏事受到惩罚,我们要说:"You deserve it." 就是"**你活该**"的意思。

—What? I just found out Jason has five million followers. I missed out on such a good party.
—You deserve it.
—Aw…

这个夸张的英文表达你一定要学会！

A: Hey, man, even though I made you into an Internet celebrity, don't change who you are.
D: I'll never change. I'm just a prairie boy.
A: I really hope you don't become a bad person.
D: I'm the same down-to-earth guy. I promise.
A: Okay, good. Wanna have dinner with the company tonight?
D: What? I'm a celebrity! I only have dinner with supermodels, bro.
A: Oh, God, **I've created a monster**.

OK, 听完今天的对话之后，我们要来学习的表达是："I've created a monster."

Ya, we usually say "Oh, God, **I've created a monster.**" **It's usually a bad thing**. I think this comes from maybe science fiction（科幻）movies or books. Maybe if a doctor wants to create something to help people, but it becomes something very bad. Like frankenstein（科学怪人）for example, we can say, "Oh, God, I've created a monster."

So in this case, Alex want to help me to become an Internet celebrity, but he didn't want me to change who I was. If I become really really arrogant, and think I'm better than everyone else, and I become a bad person, he could say, "Oh, God, I've created a monster."

OK，在口语中，如果我们用这句话，"I've created a monster."其实是有点儿夸张的。比如说，我把大白变成网红之后，他就开始自我膨胀，这个时候我就可以对自己说，"I've created a monster."他是不是真的变成了 monster 呢？其实不是。这是一种比较夸张的手法，即"我创造了一个怪物，我创造了一个魔鬼。"

OK, so for the bonus, you heard me say, I'm the down-to-earth guy. "**Down-to-earth**" means that **you stay humble, usually with celebrities**, we think. OK, it's really good because I met this celebrity, and they are really down-to-earth. They treated me really well. They didn't have an inflated ego.

OK，"down-to-earth"跟我们前几天学习的"inflated ego"是相对的，后者是指"自我膨胀"，觉得自己成功了就了不起了，"down-to-earth"是指"脚踏实的"，比较接地气的，平易近人的。

Day 84

ass-kisser 是什么意思？

D: Hey, boss, you're the best.

A: What?

D: You're so kind and treat me so well. I'm lucky.

A: Oh, thanks, man.

D: You're handsome too. And talented. And charming.

A: Wow, that's so kind of you.

D: Ya. So... can I take next week off?

A: You **ass-kisser**! You're working next week and I'm fining you!

D: Awww...

All right，听完今天的对话之后，我们要来学习一个特别有趣的表达，"ass-kisser"。

"Ass-kisser", it doesn't actually mean you're kissing somebody's ass. It just means **you flatter somebody.** If you kiss somebody's ass, it means that you flatter someone. You say a bunch of nice things to someone because you want something in return.

So for example, I compliment the boss. I say a bunch of nice things because I want to take a week off. You can say, I'm kissing my boss's ass.

OK，大家都知道，"ass"是"屁股"的意思，"kisser"是"亲吻者"，"ass-kisser"放到一起不是去亲某人的屁股，而是"拍马屁"，"ass-kisser"就是拍马屁的人。去拍某人的马屁怎么说呢？叫作"kiss somebody's ass"。

OK, so for the bonus, if you are a worker and you ask for a leave, you can say, "**Can I take the day off?**", "Can I take the week off?", "Can I take the month off?". To "take a day off" means not to work for that day.

今天的bonus部分我们学习了一个有关"请假"的标准说法，叫"Can I take+时间段+off?"。比如说："明天我能请假吗？"就可以说"Can I take tomorrow off?"

—Alex, I have 1.8 million fans. I don't wanna work today. I'm taking the day off.
—Shut up. I'm fining you.
—Aw.

这样表达"抢了某人的风头"非常地道！

A：Darby, we're hiring a new foreign teacher.

D：Oh, really?

A：Ya. He's from England. He's really tall and super handsome.

D：What? No! He'll **steal my thunder**!

A：Don't worry. You're more handsome than him.

D：Really?

A：Just kidding! He's way more handsome. And he has a 6-pack too.

D：That's it! I quit!

A：Haha.

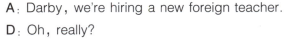

OK, 听完今天的对话之后，我们要来学习一个非常地道的表达，"steal my thunder"。

If someone **steals your thunder**, it means **maybe at first, you're the center of the attention, you're the most important person, but then they come, and everybody stops caring about you, and cares more about them.**

So in this conversation, I'm the only foreign teacher right now at 优乐说. If a more handsome teacher comes, and becomes more popular than me. I could say, aw, he stole my thunder.

"steal one's thunder" 的意思就是"抢了某人的风头"。大白是我们"Yolo Talk"唯一的外教，如果有一个比他还帅的外教来授课，他就会觉得抢了他的风头。

OK, so for today's bonus, we will teach you another expression that kind of means the same thing as "steal someone's thunder".

We say to "**steal the spotlight**". This comes from theater. If you have the main actor, the spotlight, which is a light that will be focused on the main actor, but if there's a new actor or actress who's more handsome or beautiful than the other actor, they will have the spotlight on them, so we can say, they stole the spotlight.

A really good example of this is maybe when a bride is getting married, she has to choose bridesmaids, and a lot of the time the bride will want to choose bridesmaids that are less attractive than her, because she wants to be the center of the attention at her wedding. She doesn't want anyone to steal the spotlight.

今天的 bonus 当中我们学习了一个表达叫 "steal the spotlight", 是 "抢了某人的风头"。比如在结婚的时候，一般伴娘都不能比新娘漂亮，因为如果比新娘漂亮，伴娘就会 "steal the spotlight of the bride"。

—Hey, Darby, why do you always invite me out?
—Because I'm better looking than you. You can't steal my spotlight.
—Shut up! Because I'm paying the bill.

nightmare 只是"噩梦"的意思吗？

D: Aw, man. My date last night was a **nightmare**.

A: I'm sure it wasn't that bad.

D: No, it was actually a nightmare.

A: What happened?

D: I spilt wine all over her new bag.

A: Man. That's just an accident. It's okay.

D: No, it's not okay. It's a disaster.

A: Why?

D: The bag… was Louis Vuitton.

A: Uh, oh… but maybe it's fake…

D: Ya, true, she didn't slap me…

A: Haha.

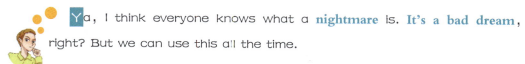

All right，听完今天的对话之后，我们要来学习一个非常地道的表达，而且特别实用，叫"**nightmare**"。

Ya, I think everyone knows what a **nightmare** is. **It's a bad dream**, right? But we can use this all the time.

Say you go on a trip, and it's raining the whole time, and you get sick, and it's a big waste of money. You can say it was a nightmare.

Say you're teaching a class, and the students are very naughty, and it's terrible. You can say, that class was a nightmare.

"nightmare" 原意是 "噩梦"，在英语口语中指的是 "不好的经历"，你可以说："It was a nightmare." "That was a nightmare."

OK, so for today's bonus, you heard me say at the end of the conversation, "She didn't **slap** me." So what does slap mean? It means you have an open hand, and you **hit somebody in the face**. (Alex：扇耳光，to slap somebody.)

—Hey, Darby, why is you face red?
—Actually, she did slap me.
—Hahaha.

Day 87

sleep 可不只是"睡觉"的意思

A: Hey, man. That hot girl asked you out!
D: Ya. She's okay…
A: Aren't you gonna go out with her?
D: I'm not sure. I haven't decided.
A: Really? But she's super cool.
D: She's okay. I don't know. I'm gonna **sleep on it** first.
A: She's really rich, you know?
D: Oh, Never mind. I like her. She'll be my girlfriend.
A: Knew it!

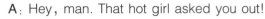

OK, 听完今天的对话之后, 我们要来学习一个非常有意思的表达叫 "sleep on it"。意思是不是 "睡在……上面" 呢?

OK, so when we say "I'm gonna sleep on it", it sounds strange, but actually what we mean is we have to make a really important decision but we don't want to make it right away, because sometimes if you make a decision too soon, you make the wrong decision.

So if we say "I'm gonna **sleep on it**", it means "**I'm gonna go to sleep, and maybe the next day I'll make the decision**". It means "**I'm gonna take some time to think about it, and the next day I'll finally make my decision**".

OK,"sleep on it"用于当你想要做一个非常重要的决定,你想花点儿时间慎重考虑一下的时候,字面意思就是我先去睡觉,第二天早上起来再给你答复,即"慎重考虑"的意思。

OK, so for the bonus, in the conversation, Alex said "She's really rich, you know?" He knows that my response is gonna be "Oh, never mind. I like her. She'll be my girlfriend." He knows me. He knows that I love money, so he says "**Knew it**." It means **he knew exactly what I was gonna say**.

For example, if Alex invited me out to drink beer, and I said "Actually you know I have been wanting to save money." And Alex says "I'm paying." I could say "Oh, ya, sure, I'll come out for beer." He could say "Ugh, knew it."

"Knew it."这个短句大家天天都可以用到,真的非常实用,译成中文可以叫:"我就知道!"其完整的句子是"I knew it."。在口语中为了简洁,就直接说"Knew it."。这样听起来更短、更酷一些。

—Hey, Alex, I'm having a party tonight, do you wanna come?
—I'm too tired, man.
—I invited a bunch of hot girls.
—I'll be there!
—Knew it!

Day 88

怎样形容一个女孩美到令人窒息？

A：My new girlfriend is **drop dead gorgeous**.

D：Nice, man. You know what else is gorgeous?

A：What?

D：My eyes!

A：Get over yourself! They're not.

D：I don't think they are, either. It's just so many girls tell me. I'm starting to believe them.

A：You're the worst!

D：Hahaha!

OK，听完今天的对话之后，我们要来学习一个非常高级的表达叫"drop dead gorgeous"。

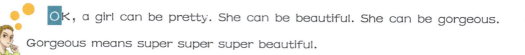

OK, a girl can be pretty. She can be beautiful. She can be gorgeous. Gorgeous means super super super beautiful.

If you wanna say she's even more beautiful than gorgeous, you can say **drop dead gorgeous**. It literally means she is so gorgeous that you can just ... you'll die. You have a heart attack. Allow me to 炫耀我的中文：**倾国倾城**.

如果你要形容一个女孩漂亮，你可以用 beautiful，稍微夸张一点儿，你可以叫 beautiful（语气加重）。比 beautiful 程度更高的词叫什么呢？叫 gorgeous。大家注意这个单词的发音，很多同学都读不好，前面 gor 是要卷舌的，后面不卷舌。 gorgeous（范读）。

比 gorgeous 程度还要高，比 gorgeous 还要漂亮，那叫什么呢？ 叫 **drop dead gorgeous**。 用大白的话来说就是"倾国倾城"。你看到她的美貌感觉心脏病都要犯了，"哐"地一下倒地了。

All right, for today's bonus. You just learned that drop dead gorgeous means really really beautiful. There's another expression you can use. You can say **breathtakingly gorgeous**. It means that **the girl is so beautiful, so gorgeous, that she actually takes your breath away**. You can't even breathe if you see her. Allow me to 炫耀我的中文：沉鱼落雁。

OK，**breathtakingly gorgeous**，大家想一想：breath 是"呼吸"的意思，take 是把你的呼吸都拿走了，中文有一个词叫"**美到窒息**"，其对应的英文就是 breathtakingly gorgeous。（大白：亭亭玉立。）

—Hey, Darby, you know who is drop dead gorgeous?
—I don't know who, but I know what. My eyes.
—Shut up!

177

Day 89

又一个安慰人的地道表达你一定要 *get*！

D：Man, I'm feeling blue.

A：What's wrong?

D：Lately I've been depressed about work. It's stressful. I work so hard every day.

A：Don't worry. **Life has its ups and downs**.

D：Ya, I guess that's true.

A：The most important thing is to stay busy.

D：Really?

A：Ya. So come to work this weekend too.

D：I knew you were gonna say that.

A：Hahaha!

All right, 听完今天的对话之后，我们要来学习一句安抚别人的话叫："Life has its ups and downs."

Yeah, exactly we use this to comfort someone. If someone is feeling blue, if someone is feeling down, we say, "Don't worry, **Life has its ups and downs**." It means **right now if you feel down, but in the future, things will get better**.

这个表达的中文意思就是："人生起起伏伏。" 因为 "ups" 就是 "上"，"downs" 就是 "下"，所以，"Life has its ups and downs." 就是 "人生起起伏伏，很正常"。我们可以用这句话去安抚那些心情不好或者事业处于低谷期的朋友们。

OK, for today's bonus. We'll teach you a really interesting expression. Sometimes we say "**Shit happens**!" It means… "shit" in this situation means some bad thing. So in this case we're saying um… **Sometimes bad things happen. Don't worry about it**.

For example, I could have a really really bad class and some students gave me a really bad evaluation. I could say, "Oh, Alex, my class was terrible. I don't wanna do it anymore." You could say, "Shit happens. Don't worry about it. Next time it will be better."

"Shit happens!" 这句话经常被一些外国的年轻人印到 T-shirt 上面来表明他们对生活的态度。不好的事情总会发生，发生了怎么办呢？ 坦然地面对就好了。安抚自己一句话，就说："Shit happens!"

—Alex, you know, I'm feeling sick, so I'm gonna take the next three days off. Shit happens, you know.
—又在装病. Shut up!

Day 90

如何用英语表达"旋风式的爱情"?

A: Man, you need to stop being so impulsive.

D: What do you mean?

A: Your last relationship… you met, dated for 1 month, got married and then got divorced.

D: Ya, I admit that was a **whirlwind romance**. That was a bad mistake.

A: You need to be more careful about falling in love.

D: Oh, speaking of falling in love. I totally have a new girlfriend.

A: Really?

D: She's the best. We're gonna get married next week.

A: You idiot.

OK, 听完今天的对话之后,我们要学习一个非常酷炫的表达。

Whirlwind romance, what's whirlwind in Chinese? (Alex: 旋风.) OK, so everyone understands. You know whirlwind, the wind moved extremely fast, so **we use this to describe a relationship that goes too fast**.

If two people meet, immediately fall in love, immediately get engaged, get married, and then maybe only a couple months later, get divorced, we say this is a "whirlwind romance". We use this especially with celebrities.

Many celebrities will meet each other, get married, and then get divorced very very quickly. We say that was whirlwind romance.

OK, **whirlwind romance** 用中文解释有点儿奇怪，即"旋风式的爱情"。形容那种来也匆匆去也匆匆的爱情关系。

OK, for today's bonus. The word is "**impulsive**". It's an adjective and it means that **you don't use your brain before making a decision**. In this situation, two people decided to get married without thinking, and we could say that is impulsive. You could say "冲动的"。(Alex：Yeah，"冲动的"，impulsive.)

Yeah, so we also use this, for example, impulsive shopper. If somebody see something and just buy it without thinking about how much it costs, we could say, "You're too impulsive."

"impulsive shopper"指的就是那种冲动型的消费者，在我们身边肯定有这样的人，买东西很冲动，买了以后却发现用不着。

—Hey, Alex, I just bought a boxing ring for my apartment.
—What? Do you have a boxing partner?
—Uh…
—You impulsive idiot!

"对某人有感觉"可以这样表达！

D: Boss, I **have** the biggest **crush on** a new girl.
A: Oh, really?
D: We are totally gonna fall in love.
A: Why do you think that?
D: This girl I met on the internet let me take her to her favorite bar and buy her 3 bottles of wine.
A: Um… and then?
D: Suddenly she had to leave. She said her grandpa was in the hospital. Poor girl.
A: Um… how much did you spend on her?
D: Just like 6,000 RMB. I can't wait for her to call me today.
A: Hmmm… interesting.

OK，听完今天的对话之后，我们要来学习一个非常地道的表达叫"have a crush on"。

Yeah, if you **have a crush on someone**. It means that **you kind of like them. It doesn't mean that you love them, it just means that you're thinking about them**.

Actually we often use this for teenagers, because teenagers don't know what real love is. Right?

So if a 14-or 15-year-old says, "Oh, my God! I love this girl or I love this guy." We say that's not real love. You just have a crush on that person. It means you like them.

OK,"have a crush on somebody"翻译成中文就是"对某人有感觉"。

And we actually often use this expression, if somebody likes someone, but they're too shy, or they're too scared to tell them, so they secretly like someone. They have a crush on them, but the other person doesn't know.

So, for today's bonus. We have another expression that we use a lot: **secret admirer**. It means **somebody that secretly likes you, but is too scared to tell you**. We say you have a secret admirer.

—OK,就是"暗恋者",secret admirer.

—I have so many.

—Get over yourself.

—Boss, the girl from last night at the bar, she hasn't called me yet.

—Knew it.

—Awww…

sit shotgun 这个表达非常有趣!

D: Wow. Nice car, boss! I'm **sitting shotgun**!

A: Ya, man, Ferrari.

D: I love it!

A: Darby, work harder this year.

D: Of course, boss. Obviously I'm gonna work so hard.

A: So that next year I can buy a new car.

D: I hate you. I quit.

A: Hahaha.

All right, 听完今天的对话之后，我们要来学习一个非常有趣的表达叫 "sit shotgun"。

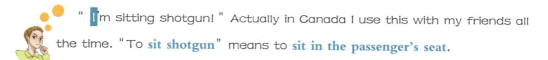

"I'm sitting shotgun!" Actually in Canada I use this with my friends all the time. "To **sit shotgun**" means to **sit in the passenger's seat**.

OK, why do we say this? Because in the past, there were horse carriages. Someone would hold the horses, and the person beside them in the passenger's seat will hold the gun to keep the horse carriage safe. So we say "sit shotgun" means to sit in the passenger's seat.

"sit shotgun" 这个表达指的是：坐在副驾驶这个位置上。它来源于什么呢？很久以前，美国有一种马车，驾驶马车的那个人旁边一般会有一个人拿着猎枪（shotgun）去保护这辆马车以及驾马车的人。所以后来引申意就是：当表达你 sit shotgun 的时候就是说你坐在副驾驶上。

As today's bonus, we're gonna teach you another expression that has to do with driving, that has to do with cars. It's "**road rage**". OK, so we know what a road is, and rage means anger.

So what "road rage" is…is **people getting extremely angry when they are driving**. You might see videos online of people that are so angry at other drivers that they actually get out of the car and they start fighting with each other. We call this "road rage".

In America, for example, in the United States, a lot of people have guns in their cars. Some people gets so angry at other drivers, and they actually take out their guns and start shooting at each other.

"road rage" 翻译成中文就是 "路怒"。所以大家开车的时候一定要心平气和，不要生气，因为情绪激动就容易出事故。

bread 和 *butter*
组合起来会有什么新的意思呢？

A: Darby, the students love you.

D: Ya, man. I'm not a great actor. Teaching is my **bread and butter**.

A: You're the best foreign teacher in China.

D: Thanks, man. I appreciate that.

A: When I found you on the Internet, nobody cared about you.

D: No! I had 2,000 followers.

A: How many do you have now?

D: 2 million.

A: You're welcome.

OK，听完今天的对话之后，我们要来学习一个很地道的表达，叫作"bread and butter"。

Ya, we use "**bread and butter**" to describe the main thing that we are good at, the main thing that we use to make a living, to put food on our table, to pay for everything we have in our life.

This comes from back in history. People pretty much only had bread to eat, "bread and butter", right? So you use your main skill to buy bread and butter so that you could stay alive.

So for me, if I say I'm not really a great actor, that's not my bread and butter. My bread and butter's teaching. That's what I do.

OK,"bread and butter"原意指的是"面包和黄油",现在的引申义是自己的"看家本领",比如说对于老师来说,"Teaching is their bread and butter."对于演员来说,"Acting is their bread and butter."什么是你的看家本领,(什么)就是你的"bread and butter"。

OK, so for today's bonus. In today's conversation, you heard Alex say "You're welcome", but I never say "Thank you!" **If you use "You're welcome" without somebody saying "Thank you", it's a kind of sarcastic way of saying "You should thank me."**

So in this situation, I only had two thousand followers before, Alex helped me to get two million fans two million followers, but I didn't say "Thank you", but he thinks I should say "Thank you", so he says "You're welcome."

"You're welcome."这个表达大家肯定都知道,就是当别人说了"Thank you!"之后你会说"You're welcome."(不用谢)。但是在电影和美剧里大家经常可以看到另外一种用法:当你认为对方应该谢谢你的时候,你就直接来一句:"You're welcome."

—Hey, Alex, I've improved myself so much over the last year.
—You're welcome.
—It's not because of you. It's because of me,好吗?

学会用这个表达去夸你的女朋友!

D: Boss, sometimes I think you just hired me to be a cash cow.

A: No way, man. You're a good friend. I don't use you for money.

D: Okay. Thanks. That's a relief.

A: Oh, we have a business dinner tonight.

D: Should I come?

A: Ya, but don't do any talking. Just sit there, smile and look handsome.

D: What? You just hired me to be **eye candy**!

A: Ya... pretty much. You should be proud.

D: Actually I kind of am. I totally am eye candy.

A: OK, get over yourself...

OK, 听完今天的对话之后, 我们要学习一个非常漂亮的表达叫 "eye candy"。

"Eye candy", so we know what an eye is, and we know what candy is, so it means **something that when you look at it, it's very sweet.** (Alex: So sweet!) It's very beautiful. OK, so this word can be...it can have a good meaning, and it can also have a bad meaning.

For example, if a boss hires a really really beautiful girl, but maybe she doesn't really have much skill or talent. You could say the boss just hired her to be eye candy, just someone to look at, because they're beautiful.

But it can also be used in a good way. You can say, "Wow, someone is eye candy." That's actually a compliment. It means when you look at them, they're very beautiful, and you like looking at them.

"eye candy" 指的就是那些看了让人觉得赏心悦目的人，长得很好看的人。你可以把它用作贬义，比如说"她就是个花瓶"：She's just eye candy. 当然它也可以用来夸别人，你可以说你的女朋友是 eye candy。

OK, for today's bonus. We'll just teach you a very useful expression. Wow, **that's a relief**. If you are really really worried about something, but then turns out you have nothing to worry about. You can say, "That's a relief."

OK, "That's a relief." 的意思就是："终于让我放心了。" That's a relief.

For example, in school, if you have to make a really really big presentation, and you're really really nervous about it, then you find out actually it's canceled, and you don't have to make the presentation. Ah…that's a relief.

—Darby, you don't have to work tomorrow.
—Really? Wow, thanks. That's such a relief!
—Just kidding.
—I hate you.

怎样洋气地表达"适可而止"?

D: Ugh, I'm so tired.

A: What's wrong?

D: I just lifted weights for 3 hours.

A: Dude, that's too long.

D: Ya. I feel like I'm gonna die.

A: Remember, **everything in moderation**. You need to have balance in life.

D: Okay. What did you do last night?

A: Oh, I didn't sleep. I played video games for 14 hours.

D: Um… what were you saying about moderation?

All right,听完今天的对话之后,我们要来学习一个非常洋气的表达叫"everything in moderation"。

Yeah, we always say "everything in moderation". It's a healthy way to live your life. It means…what moderation means not too much of anything.

For example, if you drink beer, and you drink one bottle, that's moderation. If you drink twenty bottles, that's too much, right? If you go to the gym, and you run for three hours, that's too much. We say just run for twenty minutes or half an hour. So **everything in moderation** means **don't do too much of anything**. If…I can 炫耀我的中文:适可而止.

对,"适可而止",或者是"凡事都有个度",everything in moderation。

All right, so it's time for today's bonus. We say "everything in moderation", because you shouldn't do things excessively. The word "**excessive**" means **too much**.

If you drink twenty beers, that's excessive. It's bad for your health. If you go to the gym for three hours, you could hurt yourself, because it's excessive. It means"过度"。

OK,今天的 bonus 当中我们学习了一个跟 everything in moderation 相对的词,就是"过度的"——excessive。如果你喝一瓶啤酒,可能比较适度,或者喝两瓶也 OK。但你突然喝二十瓶,那就叫什么呢? (大白:Excessive drinking.) Yeah.

—Darby, how many coffees did you drink today?
—Oh, this is just like my eight cups.

191

Day 96

"拜金主义者"用英语怎么说？

D: Boss, I have a new girlfriend.
A: Really? Again?
D: Ya. She treats me so well.
A: How old is she?
D: She's like... um... she's... uh...
A: Dude! She had better not be under-aged.
D: Um... she's 55.
A: 55? But you're just 29.
D: Hey, man! I'll be thirty soon. Plus, she's really rich.
A: You're such a **gold digger**. Get out of here.

All right，听完今天的对话之后，我们要来学习一个非常地道的表达 "gold digger"。

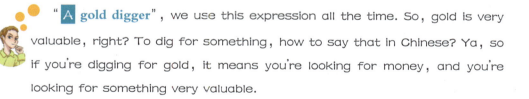

"**A gold digger**", we use this expression all the time. So, gold is very valuable, right? To dig for something, how to say that in Chinese? Ya, so if you're digging for gold, it means you're looking for money, and you're looking for something very valuable.

So, for example, **if there's a 20 year old boy or a 20 year old girl, and they're dating someone way older than them, but that person is really really rich, we could say they're just dating that person for the money. They're gold digger.**

"gold digger" 用中文说就是**拜金主义者**，只看对方的钱就跟对方去 date 的人。

All right, so for today's bonus. We just taught you "gold digger", someone who is looking for someone with a lot of money, but for example, **if there's a 50 or 60 year old man or woman and they're dating someone who is very very young but attractive**, we could say that they're a **sugar daddy** or **sugar mama**.

So if I said I wanna find a sugar mama, it means, allow me to 炫耀我的中文：我想吃软饭。

你想吃软饭？不给。OK，"sugar daddy" 其实就是我们说的那种打引号的"干爹"，"sugar mama" 就是那种打引号的"富婆妈妈"。

—I wanna find true love, Alex.
—OK.
—Do you know any older women that have lots of money?
—That's not true love. You gold digger, Darby.

Day 97

如何形容那些特别努力的人？

D: Man, we're the best team ever.

A: Obviously. We always **give 110%**!

D: We work day and night!

A: No one works harder than us!

D: Alright, so let's get to work.

A: Actually I'm a little tired. Maybe we should have a break.

D: You know what, me too. Let's take the afternoon off. I wanna go home and sleep.

A: Good idea. I'm gonna lie in bed and play video games.

D: See ya, man.

A: Ya, see ya tomorrow or the next day maybe.

All right, 听完这段对话之后，我们要来学习一个跟数字相关的很地道的表达叫作 "**give 110%**"。

Yeah, we use this all the time if we wanna show how much effort we gonna use to do something. It makes sense to say give 100% that means to put all of your effort, 100% of your effort into something.

But if we say **give 110%**, it means **all my effort plus even more effort. It exaggerates, and it means we gonna work our very hardest to do something**. I could say I'm gonna train for some kind of sports tenement. I'm gonna give 110%. I'm gonna be in the gym every day.

我们在做某件事情的时候，能付出100%的努力，就已经很厉害了。而对话中的表达是110%，就是你付出比100%还要多的努力，那是不是更厉害呢？

All right, so for today's bonus. In the conversation we said, "**We work day and night.**" "Day and night" means that **we work all the time, constantly working**.

There is another expression that exaggerates the amount of work that you do. You can say I feel like I **work 24/7**. That's 24 hours a day, 7 days a week, **working all the times**. So if someone works 24/7, it means that they work extremely hard.

OK，今天的 bonus 学习了两个表达。一个是"We work day and night."，就是不分昼夜地工作。还有一个更夸张的表达是什么呢？"We work 24/7." 在"24"之后划一根斜线，然后再写上"7"。

"24"代表一天24小时，"7"代表的是一周7天，就是从不间断地工作。"I work 24/7."说明完全没有休息，一直在工作。

Now maybe you guys don't know but Alex and I put 110% into going to the gym everyday. So, let's go.

—Emmm...I'm sorry, Darby, I have to go back home and cook dinner.
—Oh...Yeah, I forgot I need to...wash my cloths.
—OK, bye！
—Bye-bye！

Day 98

年轻人都会用到的一个表达！

D: Man, yesterday was the worst day ever!

A: What happened?

D: I worked hard all day. I tripped on my way home and hurt my knee.

A: Wow. That's rough.

D: And then when I got home, my cat had peed on my bed. **FML**.

A: Dude, I agree. Your life sucks.

D: Ya. So I know today will be better.

A: Of course. Just remember you promised to work overtime tonight.

D: F…M…

A: Haha.

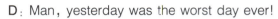

All right，听完今天的对话之后，我们来学习一个非常洋气的表达叫"**FML**"，几乎所有的年轻人都会用到它。

This is super popular right now to say **FML**. If you're having a terrible day, everything is going wrong, you can say FML. What it stands for… is … the F…is… I can't say it. It's the "F" word. You guys…you guys probably know. "M" is "my", and "L" is "life". So it means **F My Life**.

In other words, **my life sucks**. In the conversation, a bunch of really bad things happened to me in one day, So I said, "FML."

"FML"是时下非常流行的一个地道的表达方式。它其实由三个单词组成，第一个单词就是"F" word，第二个是"My"，第三个是"Life"，F My Life。这个表达在什么时候用呢？比如说你今天遇到的事都不是很顺，那你就会说"FML"。

Now, you just learned FML. If everything is going bad, you can say, "Ugh…FML." There's another older expression but we still use it. We say, "**When it rains it pours**." That means if there's a little bit of rain, a lot of rain will come.

So in other words, allow me to 炫耀我的中文：祸不单行．（Alex：Yeah, right. Say that English again.）"When it rains it pours."

—Ugh…It's six o'clock, finally time to go home.
—Darby, you have class tonight.
—Oh, FML.
—Hahaha.

comfort food 这个可爱的表达是什么意思呢？

D: Dude. You're having 2 burgers and ice cream for lunch. That's so much!

A: It's **comfort food**. My girlfriend broke up with me.

D: Ya, but you're getting fat.

A: What?

D: Good luck finding a new girlfriend.

A: OMG... I'm so sad! Another burger, please! With extra sauce!

D: Hahaha.

OK，听完今天的对话之后，我们要学习一个非常可爱的表达叫"comfort food"。

Yeah, **Comfort food**. "comfort" means "安慰". (Alex: Yeah.) Sorry, I always like to show off my Chinese. If you eat food to comfort yourself. Some people do this. (Alex: 嗯哼！) **If they feel stressed or if they feel sad, they'll go and they'll eat a bunch of food.**

Sometimes if you watch a movie and there's a girl and she just got dumped by her boyfriend. (Alex: 嗯哼！) And you see that she has a big bucket of ice cream and she's eating the ice cream and crying. We can say that she's eating comfort food. She's eating food to make herself feel better.

OK,"comfort food"就是<u>当你心情不好的时候</u>,比如说你被你老板骂了,或者是你跟你的女朋友分手了,或者是你的小猫不见了……<u>你要去吃点东西去安抚一下自己</u>,这个时候你就可以用"comfort food"。

All right, so for today's bonus. A similar expression is "to **pig out**". **If something bad happens, if you feel really stressed, if you feel really sad**, you wanna eat comfort food. So we can also say **you pig out on food**. This is a verb.

In English we say to eat like a pig. It means to eat eat eat eat eat too much. So if you pig out, it means 3 burgers, french fries, ice cream, pigging out.

OK,"pig out"指的是"<u>大吃特吃</u>"。比如说你花 500 块钱要去吃一个自助餐,然后你说:"I'm gonna pig out."

—Now,大白老师,I would never pig out.(Alex:Ya, sure.)I watch my diet.

—Yeah. Totally. So, what would you have for dinner?

—I'm gonna eat a whole pizza.

—Haha…

"开心又难过"这种复杂的心情怎么表达？

D: Man. I'm emotional today.
A: Why's that?
D: This is the 100th class. After this we're done.
A: Ya. I feel the same. It's **bittersweet**.
D: It's nice to be finished, but it's been a lot of fun recording this course with you.
A: Totally bittersweet. But the most important thing is that our awesome fans enjoy the course.
D: Ya. That's true. Congratulations everyone on completing the course!
A: You made it to 100 days! Thank you for your support.
D: Congratulations, guys!
A: Congratulations!

———◯◯———

OK, 听完今天的对话之后，我们来学习一个非常高级的表达叫"bittersweet"。

Bittersweet, it means **you have a happy feeling about something but at the same time you have a sad feeling about it**. So, you have two different feelings.

You guys just made it to 100 days, so we're so proud of you, and we're so happy for you. But, it's bitter because we're gonna miss you so much.

OK,"**bittersweet**"这个词是由"bitter"加上"sweet"组合在一起成为的一个新词。bitter 是"苦的",sweet 是"甜的"。就像大白说的,我们一起坚持学习了 100 天这个课程,如果你听到了这节课的话,"We're so proud of you.",我们为你感到骄傲,我们也为你感到开心。

但是,我们觉得难过的原因是"It's time to say goodbye."我们这本书中的全部内容就到这里了,但是没关系,我们会在你学习英文的路上一直陪伴着你。

OK,so for today's bonus. We're gonna teach you an expression "to **hold back tears**". Some people are emotional, but they don't wanna show their emotion. So even if **they want to cry, they will not allow themselves to cry**. We call that "holding back your tears".

"holding back tears" 是什么呢? 当你想哭的时候, 你硬生生地把自己的眼泪憋回去。"Holding back your tears."

—Darby, why are you crying?
—I can't hold back my tears anymore.
—Thank you, guys! We're gonna miss you!
—Miss you!
—Oh, by the way, see you in Season 2.
—第二季见啦!Bye!
—Bye-bye!
—爱你们!

# 读者精彩留言

奶嗦

我是"外教口语天天练"的学员，而且顺利按时学完了课程，这一百天的课程特别充实，我的英语口语水平也得到了很大提升。这本书是一扇通往英语学习之路的大门，它由浅入深、循序渐进地把我带到了英语趣味自学的道路上来，也增强了我的信心。特别棒！大白老师教学风格诙谐幽默，内容实用地道，可以满足不同水平的学员学习，学无止境，希望我们一路相伴。

Alison

通过这本书可以学到非常地道的英语口语表达、新鲜的词汇，最主要的是本书是中英双语讲解，英文讲解部分可以帮助提升英语思维能力。我本身就很喜欢学习英语，结合书中讲解的内容又非常生动有趣，学习效果特别明显。希望自己继续坚持下去，也希望这本书能够帮助到正走在英语学习之路上的你。

Summer

今年六月份报了"外教口语天天练"的一百天口语课程是我真正开始系统地学习英语口语的第一个网课。在这个过程中，我真切地感受到了自己英语口语发音的准确性和连贯性的提升，随之增加的还有我对英语口语学习的热情。这个课程真的非常好，每天都有老师帮我纠音并进行知识点的扩充，而且每周都会有两到三个不同的老师帮助答疑，群里的小伙伴们也都是一群英语口语学习的爱好者，虽然大家的年龄不同、职业不同、英语基础不同，但却有着同样高涨的学习热忱，非常高兴能加入到"外教口语天天练"的大家庭中，也期待有新的课程更新。听说大白老师把这门课的精华内容汇编成书即将出版，一定要买一本仔细品读。

夏至未至

跟着大白老师学习了一百天的英语口语课,每天模仿大白的语调进行跟读训练并做了笔记,整理了大白和 Alex 两位老师的对话,把重点内容和知识点归纳起来,忘了的时候再拿出来读一读,看看平时这些地道用语到底是怎么说的。现在两位老师要把课程的内容汇编成书,这对于读者来说真的是天大的福利。现在网上英语口语书琳琅满目,但我相信像大白老师这样的良心之作绝对是不可多得的好书。因为大白老师讲的都是时下国外超级流行的地道用语、帮助读者辨别容易产生歧义的英文表达,读了这本书相信你在和外国人交流时一定不会露怯。

Mia

Well begun is half done. "好的开始是成功的一半。" 我觉得"外教口语天天练"的课程真的让我感受到学习英语的乐趣,它并没那么的枯燥无味,而这一百天仅仅是一个开始。根据课程内容编写的这本书肯定会带给你前所未有的体验和收获,真心把好课好书分享给同样对英语学习感兴趣的你。

瑛

跟着大白和 Alex 两位老师学了一期,第一感觉就是真诚和真实!Alex 自然不用说,自带喜感,超级能带动课堂气氛。而当你做 imitation 和 role play 的时候,大白老师的表情和动作真的让你感觉到他仿佛就在和你面对面地交流!我觉得能录这么多期的课程真是不容易,因为它的内容全部为原创的实用对话,同时其精心选取的核心习语表达非常地道纯正,可以帮助提高你的英语口语水平不亚于外国人。如果你还没有上过大白老师的课程,可以先了解一下他们书,相信这本书可以给你带来更多惊喜,肯定会让你对英语学习产生全新的认知。